How to
PROSPER
in
HARD TIMES

ALSO AVAILABLE FROM
TARCHER SUCCESS CLASSICS

The Law of Success
Napoleon Hill

Think and Grow Rich
Napoleon Hill

Your Magic Power to Be Rich!
Napoleon Hill

As a Man Thinketh
James Allen

Acres of Diamonds
Russell H. Conwell

The Science of Getting Rich
Wallace D. Wattles

The Science of Being Great
Wallace D. Wattles

The Master Key System
Charles F. Haanel

The Secret of the Ages
Robert Collier

Public Speaking for Success
Dale Carnegie

In Tune with the Infinite
Ralph Waldo Trine

Prosperity
Charles Fillmore

A Message to Garcia
Elbert Hubbard

JEREMY P. TARCHER/PENGUIN

a member of Penguin Group (USA) Inc.

New York

How to

PROSPER

in

HARD TIMES

Blueprints for Abundance by the Greatest
Motivational Teachers of All Time

NAPOLEON HILL,
JAMES ALLEN, JOSEPH MURPHY,
GEORGE S. CLASON, AND OTHERS

JEREMY P. TARCHER/PENGUIN
Published by the Penguin Group
Penguin Group (USA) Inc., 375 Hudson Street, New York, New York 10014, USA • Penguin Group
(Canada), 90 Eglinton Avenue East, Suite 700, Toronto, Ontario M4P 2Y3, Canada (a division of Pearson
Canada Inc.) • Penguin Books Ltd, 80 Strand, London WC2R 0RL, England • Penguin Ireland,
25 St Stephen's Green, Dublin 2, Ireland (a division of Penguin Books Ltd) • Penguin Group (Australia),
250 Camberwell Road, Camberwell, Victoria 3124, Australia (a division of Pearson Australia Group
Pty Ltd) • Penguin Books India Pvt Ltd, 11 Community Centre, Panchsheel Park, New Delhi–110 017,
India • Penguin Group (NZ), 67 Apollo Drive, Rosedale, North Shore 0632, New Zealand
(a division of Pearson New Zealand Ltd) • Penguin Books (South Africa) (Pty) Ltd, 24 Sturdee Avenue,
Rosebank, Johannesburg 2196, South Africa

Penguin Books Ltd, Registered Offices: 80 Strand, London WC2R 0RL, England

Most Tarcher/Penguin books are available at special quantity discounts for bulk purchase for sales
promotions, premiums, fund-raising, and educational needs. Special books or book excerpts also can be
created to fit specific needs. For details, write Penguin Group (USA) Inc. Special Markets,
375 Hudson Street, New York, NY 10014.

ISBN 978-1-58542-755-0

Printed in the United States of America
1 3 5 7 9 10 8 6 4 2

While the author has made every effort to provide accurate telephone numbers and Internet addresses
at the time of publication, neither the publisher nor the author assumes any responsibility for errors, or
for changes that occur after publication. Further, the publisher does not have any control over and does not
assume any responsibility for author or third-party websites or their content.

Neither the publisher nor the authors is engaged in rendering professional advice or services to the
individual reader. The ideas, procedures, and suggestions contained in this book are not intended as a
substitute for consulting with a physician. All matters regarding your health require medical supervision.
Neither the author nor the publisher shall be liable or responsible for any loss or damage allegedly
arising from any information or suggestion in the book.

CONTENTS

Promise Yourself . . .

To be so strong that nothing can disturb your peace of mind.

To talk health, happiness, and prosperity to every person you meet.

To make all your friends feel that there is something worthwhile in them.

To look at the sunny side of everything and make your optimism come true.

To think only of the best, to work only for the best, and to expect only the best.

To be just as enthusiastic about the success of others as you are about your own.

To forget the mistakes of the past and press on to the greater achievements of the future.

To wear a cheerful expression at all times and give a smile to every living creature you meet.

To give so much time to improving yourself that you have no time to criticize others.

To be too large for worry, too noble for anger, too strong for fear, and too happy to permit the presence of trouble.

To think well of yourself and to proclaim this fact to the world, not in loud words, but in great deeds.

To live in the faith that the whole world is on your side, so long as you are true to the best that is in you.

—Christian D. Larson, The Optimist Creed

How to
PROSPER
in
HARD TIMES

HOW *to* ATTRACT MONEY

Joseph Murphy

CONTENTS

YOUR RIGHT TO BE RICH

It is your right to be rich. You are here to lead the abundant life, and be happy, radiant, and free. You should, therefore, have all the money you need to lead a full, happy, prosperous life.

There is no virtue in poverty; the latter is a mental disease, and it should be abolished from the face of the earth. You are here to grow, expand, and unfold, spiritually, mentally, and materially. You have the inalienable right to fully develop and express yourself along all lines. You should surround yourself with beauty and luxury.

Why be satisfied with just enough to go around when you can enjoy the riches of the Infinite? In this book you will learn to make friends with money, and you will always have a surplus. Your desire to be rich is a desire for a fuller, happier, more wonderful life. It is a cosmic urge. It is good and very good.

Begin to see money in its true significance—as a symbol of exchange. It means to you freedom from want, beauty, luxury, abundance, and refinement.

As you read this chapter, you are probably saying, "I want more money." "I am worthy of a higher salary than I am receiving."

I believe most people are inadequately compensated. One of the causes many people do not have more money is that they are silently or openly condemning it. They refer to money as "filthy lucre," or "Love of money is the root of all evil," etc. Another reason they do not prosper is that they have a sneaky, subconscious feeling there is some virtue in poverty; this subconscious pattern may be due to early childhood training, superstition, or it could be based on a false interpretation of the scriptures.

There is no virtue in poverty; it is a disease like any other mental disease. If you were physically ill, you would think there was something wrong with you; you would seek help, or do something about the condition at once. Likewise if you do not have money constantly circulating in your life, there is something radically wrong with you.

Money is only a symbol; it has taken many forms as a medium of exchange down through the centuries, such as salt, beads, and trinkets of various kinds. In early times man's wealth was determined by the number of sheep or oxen he had. It is much more convenient to write a check than to carry some sheep around with you to pay your bills.

God does not want you to live in a hovel or go hungry. God *wants* you to be happy, prosperous, and successful. God is always successful in all His undertakings, whether He makes a star or a cosmos!

You may wish to make a trip around the world, study art in foreign countries, go to college, or send your children to a superior school. You certainly wish to bring your children up in lovely surroundings, so that they might learn to appreciate beauty, order, symmetry, and proportion.

You were born to succeed, to win, to conquer all difficulties, and have all your faculties fully developed. If there is financial lack in your life, do something about it.

Get away immediately from all superstitious beliefs about money. Do not ever regard money as evil or filthy. If you do, you cause it to take wings and fly away from you. Remember that you lose what you condemn.

Suppose, for example, you found gold, silver, lead, copper, or iron in the ground. Would you pronounce these things evil? God pronounced all things good. The evil comes from man's darkened understanding, from his unillumined mind, from his false interpretation of life, and his misuse of Divine Power. Uranium, lead, or some other metal could have been used as a medium of exchange. We use paper bills, checks, etc.; surely the piece of paper is not evil; neither is the check. Physicists and scientists know today that the only difference between one metal and another is the number and rate of motion of the electrons revolving around a central nucleus. They are now changing one metal into another through a bombardment of the atoms in the powerful cyclotron. Gold under certain conditions becomes mercury. It will only be a little while until gold, silver, and other metals will be made synthetically in the chemical laboratory. I cannot imagine seeing anything evil in electrons, neutrons, protons, and isotopes.

The piece of paper in your pocket is composed of electrons and protons arranged differently; their number and rate of motion is different; that is the only way the paper differs from the silver in your pocket.

Some people will say, "Oh, people kill for money. They steal for money!" It has been associated with countless crimes, but that does not make it evil.

A man may give another $50 to kill someone; he has misused money in using it for a destructive purpose. You can use electricity to kill someone or light the house. You can use water to quench the baby's thirst, or use it to drown the child. You can use fire to warm the child, or burn it to death.

Another illustration would be if you brought some earth from your garden, put it in your coffee cup for breakfast, that would be your evil; yet the earth is not evil; neither is the coffee. The earth is displaced; it belongs in your garden.

Similarly if a needle were stuck in your thumb, it would be your evil; the needle or pin belongs in the pin cushion, not in your thumb.

We know the forces or the elements of nature are not

evil; it depends on our use of them whether they bless or hurt us.

A man said to me one time, "I am broke. I do not like money; it is the root of all evil."

Love of money to the exclusion of everything else will cause you to become lopsided and unbalanced. You are here to use your power or authority wisely. Some men crave power; others crave money. If you set your heart on money, and say, "That is all I want. I am going to give all my attention to amassing money; nothing else matters," you can get money and attain a fortune, but you have forgotten that you are here to lead a balanced life. "Man does not live by bread alone."

For example, if you belong to some cult, or religious group, and become fanatical about it, excluding yourself from your friends, society, and social activities, you will become unbalanced, inhibited, and frustrated. Nature insists on a balance. If all your time is devoted to external things and possessions, you will find yourself hungry for peace of mind, harmony, love, joy, or perfect health. You will find you cannot buy anything that is real. You can amass a fortune, or have millions of dollars; this is not evil or bad. Love of money to the exclusion of everything else results in frustration, disappointment, and disillusionment; in that sense it is the root of your evil.

By making money your sole aim, you simply made a wrong choice. You thought that was all you wanted, but you found after all your efforts that it was not only the money you needed. What you really desired was true place, peace of mind, and abundance. You could have the million or many millions, if you wanted them, and still have peace of mind, harmony, perfect health, and Divine expression.

Everyone wants enough money, and not just enough to go around. He wants abundance and to spare; he should have it. The urges, desires, and impulses we have for food, clothing, homes, better means of transportation, expression, procreation, and abundance are all God-given, Divine, and good, but we may misdirect these impulses, desires, and urges resulting in evil or negative experiences in our lives.

Man does not have an evil nature; there is no evil nature in you; it is God, the Universal Wisdom, or Life seeking expression through you.

For example, a boy wants to go to college, but he does not have enough money. He sees other boys in the neighborhood going off to college and the university; his desire increases. He says to himself, "I want an education, too." Such a youth may steal and embezzle money for the purpose of going to college. The desire to go to college was basically and fundamentally good; he misdirected that desire or urge by violating the laws of society, the cosmic law of harmony, or the golden rule; then he finds himself in trouble.

However, if this boy knew the laws of mind, and his unqualified capacity through the use of the Spiritual Power to go to college, he would be free and not in jail.

Who put him in jail? He placed himself there. The policeman who locked him up in prison was an instrument of the man-made laws which he violated. He first imprisoned himself in his mind by stealing and hurting others. Fear and a guilt consciousness followed; this is the prison of the mind followed by the prison walls made of bricks and stones.

Money is a symbol of God's opulence, beauty, refinement, and abundance, and it should be used wisely, judiciously, and constructively to bless humanity in countless ways. It is merely a symbol of the economic health of the nation. When your blood is circulating freely, you are healthy. When money is circulating freely in your life, you are economically healthy. When people begin to hoard money, to put it away in tin boxes, and become charged with fear, there is economic illness.

The crash of 1929 was a psychological panic; it was fear seizing the minds of people everywhere. It was a sort of negative, hypnotic spell.

You are living in a subjective and objective world. You must not neglect the spiritual food, such as peace of mind, love, beauty, harmony, joy, and laughter.

Knowledge of the spiritual power is the means to the Royal Road to Riches of all kinds, whether your desire is spiritual, mental, or material. The student of the laws of mind, or the student of the spiritual principle, believes and knows absolutely that regardless of the economic situation, stock market fluctuation, depression, strikes, war, other conditions, or circumstances, he will always be amply supplied regardless of what form money may take. The reason for this is he abides in the consciousness of wealth. The student has convinced himself in his mind that wealth is forever flowing freely in his life, and that there is always a Divine surplus. Should there be a war tomorrow, and all the student's present holdings become valueless, as the German marks did after the First World War, he would still attract wealth, and be cared for regardless of the form the new currency took.

Wealth is a state of consciousness; it is a mind conditioned to Divine supply forever flowing. The scientific thinker looks at money or wealth like the tide; i.e., it goes out, but it always comes back. The tides never fail; neither will man's supply when he trusts a tireless, changeless, immortal Presence which is Omnipresent, and flows ceaselessly. The man who knows the workings of the subconscious mind is never, therefore, worried about the economic situation, stock market panics, devaluation, or inflation of currency, since he abides in the consciousness of God's eternal supply. Such a man is always supplied and watched over by an over-shadowing Presence. "Behold the birds of the air: for they sow not, neither do they reap, gather into barns; yet your heavenly Father feedeth them. Are you not much better than they?"

As you consciously commune with the Divine-Presence claiming and knowing that It leads and guides you in all your ways, that It is a Lamp unto your feet, and a Light on your path, you will be Divinely prospered and sustained beyond your wildest dreams.

Here is a simple way for you to impress your subconscious mind with the idea of constant supply or wealth: Quiet the wheels of your mind. Relax! Let go! Immobilize the attention. Get into a sleepy, drowsy, meditative state of mind; this reduces effort to the minimum; then in a quiet, relaxed, passive way reflect on the following simple truths. Ask yourself: Where do ideas come from? Where does wealth come from? Where did you come from? Where did your brain and your mind come from? You will be led back to the One Source.

You find yourself on a spiritual, working basis now. It will no longer insult your intelligence to realize that wealth is a state of mind. Take this little phrase; repeat it slowly four or five minutes three or four times a day quietly to yourself, particularly before you go to sleep: "Money is forever circulating freely in my life, and there is always a Divine surplus." As you do this regularly and systematically, the idea of wealth will be conveyed to your deeper mind, and you will develop a wealth consciousness. Idle, mechanical repetition will not succeed in building the consciousness of wealth. Begin to feel the truth of what you affirm. You know what you are doing, and why you are doing it. You know your deeper self is responsive to what you consciously accept as true.

In the beginning people who are in financial difficulties do not get results with such affirmations as "I am wealthy," "I am prosperous," "I am successful"; such statements may cause their conditions to get worse. The reason is the subconscious mind will only accept the dominant of two ideas, or the dominant mood of feeling. When they say, "I am prosperous," their feeling of lack is greater, and something within them says, "No, you are not prosperous, you are broke." The feeling of lack is dominant so that each affirmation calls forth the mood of lack, and more lack becomes theirs. The way to overcome this for beginners is to affirm what the conscious and subconscious mind will agree on; then there will be no contradiction. Our subconscious mind accepts our beliefs, feelings, convictions, and what we consciously accept as true.

A man could engage the cooperation of his subconscious mind by saying, "I am prospering every day." "I am growing in wealth and in wisdom every day." "Every day my wealth is multiplying." "I am advancing, growing, and moving forward financially." These and similar statements would not create any conflict in the mind.

For instance if a salesman has only ten cents in his pocket, he could easily agree that he would have more tomorrow. If he sold a pair of shoes tomorrow, there is nothing within him which says his sales could not increase. He could use statements, such as, "My sales are increasing every day." "I am advancing and moving forward." He would find these would be sound psychologically, acceptable to his mind, and produce desirable fruit.

The spiritually advanced student who quietly, knowingly, and feelingly says, "I am prosperous," "I am successful," "I am wealthy," gets wonderful results also. Why would this be true? When they think, feel, or say, "I am prosperous," they mean God is All Supply or Infinite Riches, and what is true of God is true of them. When they say, "I am wealthy," they know God is Infinite Supply, the Inexchaustible, Treasure-House, and what is true of God is, therefore, true of them, for God is within them.

Many men get wonderful results by dwelling on three abstract ideas, such as health, wealth, and success. *Health* is a Divine Reality or quality of God, *Wealth* is of God; it is eternal and endless. *Success* is of God; God is always successful in all His undertakings.

The way they produce remarkable results is to stand before a mirror as they shave, and repeat for five or ten minutes: "Health, wealth, and success." They do not say, "I am healthy," or "I am successful"; they create no opposition in their minds. They are quiet and relaxed; thus the mind is receptive and passive; then they repeat these words. Amazing results follow. All they are doing is identifying with truths that are eternal, changeless, and timeless.

You can develop a wealth consciousness. Put the principles enunciated and elaborated on in this book to practice, and your desert will rejoice and blossom as the rose.

I worked with a young boy in Australia many years ago who wanted to become a physician and surgeon, but he had no money; nor had he graduated from high school. For expenses he used to clean out doctor's offices, wash windows, and do odd repair jobs. He told me that every night as he went to sleep, he used to see a diploma on a wall with his name in big, bold letters. He used to clean and shine the diplomas in the medical building where he worked; it was not hard for him to engrave the diploma in his mind and develop it there. I do not know how long he continued this imagining, but it must have been for some months.

Results followed as he persisted. One of the doctors took a great liking to this young boy, and after training him in the art of sterilizing instruments, giving hypodermic injections, and other miscellaneous first-aid work, he became a technical assistant in his office. The doctor sent him to high school and also to college at his expense.

Today this man is a prominent doctor in Montreal, Canada. He had a dream! A clear image in his mind! *His wealth was in his mind.*

Wealth is your idea, desire, talent, urge for service, capacity to give to mankind, your ability for usefulness to society, and your love for humanity in general.

This young boy operated a great law unconsciously. Troward says, "Having seen the end, you have willed the means to the realization of the end." The *end* in this boy's case was to be a physician. To imagine, see, and feel the reality of being a doctor now, to live with that idea, sustain it, nourish it, and to love it until through his imagination it penetrated the layers of the subconscious, becoming a conviction, paved the way to the fulfillment of his dreams.

He could have said, "I have no education." "I do not know the right people." "I am too old to go to school now." "I have no money; it would take years, and I am not intelligent." He would then be beaten before he started.

His wealth was in his use of the Spiritual Power within him which responded to his thought.

The means or the way in which our prayer is answered is always hidden from us except that occasionally we may intuitively perceive a part of the process. "My ways are past finding out." The *ways* are not known. The only thing man has to do is to imagine and accept the end in his mind, and leave its unfoldment to the subjective wisdom within.

Oftentimes the question is asked, "What should I do after meditating on the end and accepting my desire in consciousness? The answer is simple: You will be compelled to do whatever is necessary for the unfoldment of your ideal. The law of the subconscious is compulsion. The law of life is action and reaction. What we do is the automatic response to our inner movements of the mind, inner feeling, and conviction.

A few months ago as I went to sleep, I imagined I was reading one of my most popular books, *Magic of Faith*, in French. I began to realize and imagine this book going into all French-speaking nations. For several weeks I did this every night, falling asleep with the imaginary French edition of *Magic of Faith* in my hands.

Just before Christmas in 1954, I received a letter from a leading publisher in Paris, France, enclosing a contract drawn up, asking me to sign it, giving him permission to publish and promote abroad to all French-speaking countries the French edition of *Magic of Faith*.

You might ask me what did I do about the publishing

of this book after prayer? I would have to say, "Nothing!" The subjective wisdom took over, and brought it to pass in its own way, which was a far better way than any method I could consciously desire.

All of our external movements, motions, and actions follow the inner movements of the mind. Inner action precedes all outer action. Whatever steps you take physically, or what you seem to do objectively will all be a part of a pattern which you were compelled to fulfill.

Accepting the end wills the means to the realization of the end. Believe that you have it now, and you shall receive it.

We must cease denying our good. Realize that the only thing that keeps us from the riches that lie all around us is our mental attitude, or the way we look at God, life, and the world in general. Know, believe, and act on the positive assumption that there is no reason why you cannot have, be, and do whatever you wish to accomplish through the great laws of God.

Your knowledge of how your mind works is your saviour and redeemer. Thought and feeling are your destiny. You possess everything by right of consciousness. The consciousness of health produces health; the consciousness of wealth produces wealth. The world seems to deny or oppose what you pray for; your senses sometimes mock and laugh at you.

If you say to your friend, you are opening up a new business for yourself, he may proceed to give you all the reasons why you are bound to fail. If you are susceptible to his hypnotic spell, he may instill fear of failure in your mind. As you become aware of the spiritual power which is one and indivisible, and responds to your thought, you will reject the darkness and ignorance of the world, and know that you possess all the equipment, power, and knowledge to succeed.

To walk on the Royal Road to Riches, you must not place obstacles and impediments on the pathway of others; neither must you be jealous or envious of others. Actually when you entertain these negative states of mind, you are hurting and injuring yourself, because you are thinking and feeling it. "The suggestion," as Quimby said, "you give to another, you are giving to yourself." This is the reason that the law of the golden rule is a cosmic, divine law.

I am sure you have heard men say, "That fellow has a racket." "He is a racketeer." "He is getting money dishonestly." "He is a faker." "I knew him when he had nothing." "He is crooked, a thief, and a swindler." If you analyze the man who talks like that, he is usually in want or suffering from some financial or physical illness. Perhaps his former, college friends went up the ladder of success and excelled him; now he is bitter and envious of their progress. In many instances this is the cause of his downfall. Thinking negatively of these classmates, and condemning their wealth, causes the wealth and prosperity he is praying for to vanish and flee away. He is condemning the things he is praying for. He is praying two ways. On the one hand he is saying, "God is prospering me," and in the next breath, silently or audibly, he is saying, "I resent that fellow's wealth." Always make it a special point to bless the other person, and rejoice in his prosperity and success; when you do, you bless and prosper yourself.

If you go into the bank, and you see your competitor across the street deposit twenty times more than you do, or you see him deposit ten thousand dollars, rejoice and be exceedingly glad to see God's abundance being manifested through one of his sons. You are then blessing and exalting what you are praying for. What you bless, you multiply. What you condemn, you lose.

If you are working in a large organization, and you are silently thinking and resenting the fact you are underpaid, that you are not appreciated, and that you deserve more money and greater recognition, you are subconsciously severing your ties with that organization. You are setting a law in motion; then the superintendent or manager says to you, "We have to let you go." You dismissed yourself. The manager was simply the instrument through which your own negative, mental state was confirmed. In other words he was a messenger telling you what you conceived as true about yourself. It was an example of the law of action and reaction. The action was the internal movement of your mind; the *reaction* was the response of the outer world to conform to your inner thinking.

Perhaps as you read this, you are thinking of someone who has prospered financially by taking advantage of others, by defrauding them, in selling them unsound investments in property, etc. The answer to this is obvious, because if we rob, cheat, or defraud another, we do the same to ourselves. In reality in this case we are actually hurting or robbing from ourselves. We are in a mood of lack in the first place, which is bound to attract loss to us. The loss may come in many ways; it may come in loss of health, prestige, peace of mind, social status, sickness in the home, or in business. It may not necessarily come in loss of money. We must not be shortsighted and think that the loss has to come just in dollars and cents.

Isn't it a wonderful feeling to place your head on the pillow at night, and feel you are at peace with the whole world, and that your heart is full of goodwill toward all? There are some people who have accumulated money the wrong way, as by tramping on others, trickery, deceit, and chicanery. What is the price? Sometimes it is mental and physical disease, guilt complexes, insomnia, or hidden fears. As one man said to me, "Yes, I rode rough-shod over others. I got what I wanted, but I got cancer doing it." He realized he had attained his wealth in the wrong way.

You can be wealthy and prosperous without hurting anyone. Many men are constantly robbing themselves; they steal from themselves: peace of mind, health, joy, inspiration, happiness, and the laughter of God. They may say that they have never stolen, but is it true? Every time we resent another, or are jealous, or envious of another's wealth or success, we are stealing from ourselves. There are the thieves and robbers which Jesus cast out of the temple; likewise you must cast them out incisively and decisively. Do not let them live in your mind. Cut their heads off with the fire of right thought and feeling.

I remember in the early days of the war reading about a woman in Brooklyn, New York, who went around from store to store buying up all the coffee she could. She knew it was going to be rationed; she was full of fear that there would not be enough for her. She bought as much as she could, and stored it is the cellar. That evening she went to church services. When she came home, burglars had broken down the door, stolen not only the coffee, but silverware, money, jewelry, and other things.

This good woman said what they all say, "Why did this happen to me when I was at church? I never stole from anyone."

Is this true? Was she not in the consciousness of lack and fear when she began to hoard supplies of coffee? Her mood and fear of lack was sufficient to bring about loss in her home and possessions. She did not have to put her hand on the cash register or rob a bank; her fear of lack produced lack. This is the reason that many people who are what society calls "Good citizens" suffer loss. They are good in the worldly sense; i.e., they pay their taxes; they obey the laws, vote regularly, and are generous to charities, but they are resentful of others' possessions, their wealth, or social position. If they would like to take money when no one was looking, such an attitude is definitely and positively a state of lack, and may cause the person who indulges in such a mental state to attract charlatans or knaves who may swindle or cheat them in some business transaction.

Before the outer thief robs us, we have first robbed ourselves. There must be an inner thief, before the outer one appears.

A man can have a guilt complex, and be accusing himself constantly. I knew such a man; he was very honest as a teller in a bank. He never stole any money, but he had an illicit romance; he was supporting another woman, and denying his family. He lived in fear that he would be discovered; a deep sense of guilt resulted. Fear follows guilt. Fear causes a contraction of the muscles and mucous membranes; acute sinusitis developed. Medication only gave him temporary relief.

I explained to this client the cause of his trouble, and told him the cure was to give up his outside affair. He said he couldn't; she was his soul mate, and that he had tried. He was always condemning and accusing himself.

One day he was accused by one of the officials of the bank of having embezzled some money; it looked serious for him, as the evidence was circumstantial. He became panic stricken, and realized that the only reason he was wrongfully accused was that he had been accusing and condemning himself. He saw how the mind operates. Inasmuch as he was always accusing himself on the inner plane, he would be accused on the outer.

He broke off the relationship immediately with the other woman due to the shock of being accused of embezzling, and began to pray for Divine harmony and understanding between himself and the bank official. He began to claim, "There is nothing hidden that is not revealed. The peace of God reigns supreme in the minds and hearts of all concerned."

Truth prevailed. The whole matter was dissolved in the light of truth. Another young man was discovered as the culprit. The bank teller knew that only through prayer was he saved from a jail sentence.

The great law is: "As you would that men should think about you, think you about them in the same manner. As you would that men should feel about you, feel you also about them in like manner."

Say from your heart: "I wish for every man who walks the earth, what I wish for myself. The sincere wish of my heart is, therefore, peace, love, joy, abundance, and God's blessings to all men everywhere. Rejoice and be glad in the progression, advancement, and prosperity of all men. Whatever you claim as true for yourself, claim it for all men everywhere. If you pray for happiness and peace of mind, let your claim be peace and happiness for all. Do not ever try and deprive another of any joy. If you do, you deprive yourself. When the ship comes in for your friend, it comes in for you also.

If someone is promoted in your organization, be glad and happy. Congratulate him, rejoice in his advancement and recognition. If you are angry or resentful, you are demoting yourself. Do not try and withhold from another his God-given birthright to happiness, success, achievement, abundance, and all good things.

Jesus said, "Sow up for yourselves treasures in heaven, where the moth and the rust doth not consume, and where thieves cannot break through and steal." Hatred and resentment rot and corrode the heart causing us to become full of scars, impurities, toxins, and poisons.

The treasures of heaven are the truths of God which we possess in our soul. Fill your minds with peace, harmony, faith, joy, honesty, integrity, loving kindness, and gentleness; then you will be sowing for yourself treasures in the heavens of your own mind.

If you are seeking wisdom regarding investments, or if you are worried about your stocks or bonds, quietly claim, "Infinite Intelligence governs and watches over all my financial transactions, and whatsoever I do shall prosper." Do this frequently and you will find that your investments will be wise; moreover you will be protected from loss, as you will be prompted to sell your securities or holdings before any loss accrues to you.

Let the following prayer be used daily by you regarding your home, business, and possessions: "The overshadowing Presence which guides the planets on their course and causes the sun to shine, watches over all my possessions, home, business, and all things that are mine. God is my fortress and vault. All my possessions are secure in God. It is wonderful." By reminding yourself daily of this great truth, and by observing the laws of Love, you will always be guided, watched over, and prospered in all your ways. You will never suffer from loss, for you have chosen the Most High as your Counsellor and Guide. The envelope of God's Love surrounds, enfolds, and encompasses you at all times. You rest in the Everlasting Arms of God.

All of us should seek an inner guidance for our problems. If you have a financial problem, repeat this before you retire at night: "Now I shall sleep in peace. I have turned this matter over to the God-Wisdom within. It knows only the answer. As the sun rises in the morning, so will my answer be resurrected. I know the sunrise never fails." Then go off to sleep.

Do not fret, fuss, and fume over a problem. Night brings counsel. Sleep on it. Your intellect can not solve all your problems. Pray for the Light that is to come. Remember the dawn always comes; then the shadows flee away. Let your sleep every night be a contented bliss.

You are not a victim of circumstances, except if you believe you are. You can rise and overcome any circumstance or condition. You will have different experiences as you stand on the rock of spiritual Truth, steadfast, and faithful to your deeper purposes and desires.

In large stores, the management employs store detectives to prevent people from stealing; they catch a number every day trying to get something for nothing. All such people are living in the consciousness of lack and limitation, and are stealing from themselves, attracting at the same time all manner of loss. These people lack faith in God, and the understanding of how their minds work. If they would pray for true place, Divine expression, and supply, they would find work; then by honesty, integrity, and perseverence they would become a credit to themselves and society at large.

Jesus said, "For ye have the poor always with you' but me ye have not always." The *poor states* of consciousness are always with us in this sense, that no matter how much wealth you now have, there is something you want with all your heart. It may be a problem of health; perhaps a son or daughter needs guidance, or harmony is lacking in the home. At that moment you are poor.

We could not know what abundance was, except we were conscious of lack. "I have chosen twelve, and one of you is a devil."

Whether it be the king of England or the boy in the slums, we are all born into limitation and into the race belief. It is through these limitations we grow. We could never discover the Inner Power, except through problems and difficulties; these are our *poor states* which prod us in seeking the solution. We could not know what joy was, except we could shed a tear of sorrow. We must be aware of poverty, to seek liberation and freedom, and ascend into God's opulence.

The *poor states,* such as fear, ignorance, worry, lack, and pain, are not bad when they cause you to seek the opposite. When you get into trouble, and get kicked around from pillar to post; when you ask negative, heart-rending questions, such as "Why are all these things happened to me?" "Why does there seem to be a jinx following me?" light will come into your mind. Through your suffering, pain, or misery, you will discover the truth which sets you free. "Sweet are the uses of adversity, like a toad ugly and venomous, yet wears a precious jewel on its head."

Through dissatisfaction we are led to satisfaction. All those studying the laws of life have been dissatisfied with something. They have had some problem or difficulty which they could not solve; or they were not satisfied with the man-made answers to life's riddles. They have found their answer in the God-Presence within themselves—the pearl of great price—the precious jewel. The Bible says, "I sought the Lord, and I found him, and He delivered me from all my fears."

When you realize your ambition or desire, you will be satisfied for only a period of brief time; then the urge to expand will come again. This is Life seeking to express Itself at higher levels through you. When one desire is satisfied, another comes, etc. to infinity. You are here to grow. Life is progression; it is not static. You are here to go from glory to glory; there is no end; for there is no end to God's glory.

We are all poor in the sense we are forever seeking more light, wisdom, happiness, and greater joy out of life. God is Infinite, and never in Eternity could you exhaust the glory, beauty, and wisdom which is within; this is how wonderful you are.

In the absolute state all things are finished, but in the relative world we must awaken to that glory which was ours before the world was. No matter how wise you are, you are seeking more wisdom; so you are still poor. No matter how intelligent you are in the field of mathematics, physics, or astronomy, you are only scratching the surface. You are still poor. The journey is ever onward, upward, and Godward. It is really an awakening process, whereby you realize creation is finished. When you know God does not have to learn, grow, expand, or unfold, you begin to gradually awaken from the dream of limitation, and become alive in God. As the scales of fear, ignorance, race belief, and mass hypnosis fall from your eyes, you begin to see as God sees. The blind spots are removed; then you begin to see the world as God made it; for we begin to see it through God's eyes. Now you say, "Behold, the Kingdom of Heaven is at hand!"

Feed the "poor" within you; clothe the naked ideas, and give them form by believing in the reality of the idea, trusting the great Fabricator within to clothe it in form and objectify it. Now your word (idea) shall become flesh (take form). When you are hungry (poor states), you seek food. When worried, you seek peace. When you are sick, you seek health; when you are weak, you seek strength. Your desire for prosperity is the voice of God in you telling you that abundance is yours; therefore, through your poor state, you find the urge to grow, to expand, to unfold, to achieve, and to accomplish your desires.

A pain in your shoulder is a blessing in disguise; it tells you to do something about it at once. If there were no pain and no indication of trouble, your arm might fall off on the street. Your pain is God's alarm system telling you to seek His Peace and His Healing Power, and move from darkness to Light. When cold, you build a fire. When you are hungry, you eat. When you are in lack, enter into the mood of opulence and plenty. Imagine the end; rejoice in it. Having imagined the end, and felt it as true, you have willed the means to the realization of the end.

When you are fearful and worried, feed your mind with the great truths of God that have stood the test of time and will last forever. You can receive comfort by meditating on the great psalms. For example: "The Lord is my shepherd; I shall not want." "God is my refuge, my salvation, whom shall I fear?" "God is an ever-present help in time of trouble." "My God in Him will I trust." "He shall cover me with His feathers, and under His wings shall I rest." "One with God is a majority." "If God be for me, who can be against me?" "I do all things through Christ which strengtheneth me." Let the healing vibrations of these truths flood your mind and heart; then you will crowd out of your mind all your fears, doubts, and worries through this meditative process.

Imbibe another great spiritual truth: "A merry heart maketh a cheerful countenance." "A merry heart hath a continual feast." "A merry heart doeth good like a medicine; a broken spirit drieth the bones." "Therefore I put thee in remembrance that thou stir up the gift of God within thee." Begin *now* to stir up the gift of God by completely rejecting the evidence of senses, the tyranny and despotism of the race mind, and give complete recognition to the spiritual Power within you as the only Cause, the only Power, and the only Presence. Know that it is a responsive and beneficent Power. "Draw nigh unto it, and it will draw nigh unto you." Turn to it devotedly with assurance, trust, and love; it will respond to you as love, peace, guidance, and prosperity.

It will be your Comforter, Guide, Counsellor, and your heavenly Father. You will then say, "God is Love. I have found Him, and He truly has delivered me from all my fears. Furthermore, you will find yourself in green pastures, where abundance and all of God's riches flow freely through you.

Say to yourself freely and joyously during the day, "I walk in the consciousness of the Presence of God all day long." "His fullness flows through me at all times filling up all the empty vessels in my life."

When you are filled full of the feeling of being what you long to be, your prayer is answered. Are all the vessels full in your life? Look under health, wealth, love, and expression. Are you fully satisfied on all levels? Is there something lacking in one of these four? All that you seek, no matter what it is, comes under one of these classifications.

If you say, "All I want is truth or wisdom," you are expressing the desire of all men everywhere. That is what everyone wants, even though he or she may word it differently. Truth or wisdom is the over-all desire of every man; this comes under the classification of expression. You wish to express more and more of God here and now.

Through your lack, limitation, and problems, you grow in God's Light, and you discover yourself. There is no other way whereby you could discover yourself.

If you could not use your powers two ways, you would never discover yourself; neither would you ever deduce a law governing you. If you were compelled to be good, or compelled to love, that would not be love. You would then be an automaton. You have freedom to love, because you can give it, or retain it. If compelled to love, there is no love. Aren't you flattered when some woman tells you she loves you and wants you? She has chosen you from all the men in the world. She does not have to love you. If she were forced to love you, you would not be flattered or happy about it.

You have freedom to be a murderer or a Holy man. This is the reason that we praise such men as Lincoln and others. They decided to choose the good; we praise them for their choice. If we believe that circumstances, conditions, events, age, race, religious training, or early environment can preclude the possibility of our attaining a happy, prosperous life, we are thieves and robbers. All that is necessary to express happiness and prosperity is to *feel* happy and prosperous. The feeling of wealth produces wealth. States of consciousness manifest themselves. This is why it is said, "All that ever came before me (feeling) are thieves and robbers. Feeling is the law, and the law is the feeling.

Your desire for prosperity is really the promise of God saying that His riches are yours; accept this promise without any mental reservation.

Quimby likened prayer to that of a lawyer pleading the

case before the judge. This teacher of the laws of mind said he could prove the defendant was not guilty as charged, but that the person was a victim of lies and false beliefs. You are the judge; you render your own verdict; then you are set free. The negative thoughts of lack, poverty, and failure are all false; they are all lies; there is nothing to back them up.

You know there is only one spiritual Power, one primal cause, and you, therefore, cease giving power to conditions, circumstances, and opinions of men. Give all Power to the spiritual Power within you, knowing that It will respond to your thought of abundance and prosperity. Recognizing the supremacy of the Spirit within, and the Power of your own thought or mental image is the way to opulence, freedom, and constant supply. Accept the abundant life in your own mind. Your mental acceptance and expectancy of wealth has its own mathematics and mechanics of expression. As you enter into the mood of opulence, all things necessary for the abundant life will come to pass. You are now the judge arriving at a decision in the courthouse of your mind. You have like Quimby produced indisputable evidence showing how the laws of your mind work, and you are now free from fear. You have executed and chopped the heads off all the fear and superstitious thoughts in your mind. Fear is the signal for action; it is not really bad; it tells you to move to the opposite which is faith in God and all positive values.

Let this be your daily prayer; write it in your heart: "God is the source of my supply. That supply is my supply now. His riches flow to me freely, copiously, and abundantly. I am forever conscious of my true worth. I give of my talents freely, and I am wonderfully, divinely compensated. Thank you, Father!"

THE ROAD TO RICHES

Riches are of the mind. Let us suppose for a moment that a physician's diploma was stolen together with his office equipment. I am sure you would agree that his wealth was in his mind. He could still carry on, diagnose disease, prescribe, operate, and lecture on materia medica. Only his symbols were stolen; he could always get additional supplies. His riches were in his mental capacity, knowledge to help others, and his ability to contribute to humanity in general.

You will always be wealthy when you have an intense desire to contribute to the good of mankind. Your urge for service—i.e., to give of your talents to the world—will always find a response in the heart of the universe.

I knew a man in New York during the financial crisis of 1929, who lost everything he had including his home and all his life's savings. I met him after a lecture which I had given at one of the hotels in the city. This was what he said, "I lost everything. I made a million dollars in four years. I will make it again. All I have lost is a symbol. I can again attract the symbol of wealth in the same way as honey attracts flies."

I followed the career of this man for several years to discover the key to his success. The key may seem strange to you; yet it is a very old one. The name he gave the key was "Change water into wine!" He read this passage in the Bible, and he knew it was the answer to perfect health, happiness, peace of mind, and prosperity.

Wine in the Bible always means the realization of your desires, urges, plans, dreams, propositions, etc.; in other words it is the things you wish to accomplish, achieve, and bring forth.

Water in the Bible usually refers to your mind or consciousness. Water takes the shape of any vessel into which it is poured; likewise whatever you feel and believe as true will become manifest in your world; thus you are always changing water into wine.

The Bible was written by illumined men; it teaches practical, everyday psychology and a way of life. One of the cardinal tenets of the Bible is that you determine, mould, fashion, and shape your own destiny through right thought, feeling, and beliefs. It teaches you that you can solve any problem, overcome any situation, and that you are born to succeed, to win, and to triumph. In order to discover the Royal Road to Riches, and receive the strength and security necessary to advance in life, you must cease viewing the Bible in the traditional way.

The above man who was in a financial crisis used to say to himself frequently during the days when he was without funds, "I can change water into wine!" These words meant to him, "I can exchange the poverty ideas in my mind for the realization of my present desires or needs which are wealth and financial supply.

His mental attitude (water) was, "Once I made a fortune honestly. I will make it again (wine)." His regular affirmation consisted of, "I attracted the symbol (money) once, I am attracting it again. I know this, and feel it is true (wine)."

This man went to work as a salesman for a chemical organization. Ideas for the better promotion of their products came to him; he passed them on to his organization. It was not long until he became vice president. Within four years the company made him president. His constant mental attitude was, "I can change water into wine!"

Look upon the story in John of changing water into wine in a figurative way, and say to yourself as the above-mentioned chemical salesman did: "I can make the invisible ideas, urges, dreams, and desires of mine visible, because I have discovered a simple, universal law of mind.

The law he demonstrated is the law of action and reaction. It means your external world, body, circumstances, environment, and financial status are always a perfect reflection of your inner thinking, beliefs, feelings and convictions. This being true, you can now change your inner pattern of thought by dwelling on the idea of success, wealth, and peace of mind. As you busy your mind with these latter concepts, these ideas will gradually seep into your mentality like seeds planted in the ground. As all seeds (thoughts and ideas) grow after their kind, so will your habitual thinking and feeling manifest in prosperity, success, and peace of mind. Wise thought (action) is followed by right action (reaction).

You can acquire riches when you become aware of the fact that prayer is a marriage feast. The *feast* is a psychological one; you meditate (mentally eat of) on your good or your desire until you become *one* with it.

I will now cite a case history from my files relating how a young girl performed her first miracle in transforming "water into wine." She operated a very beautiful hair salon. Her mother became ill, and she had to devote considerable time at home, neglecting her business. During her absence two of her assistants embezzled funds. She was forced into bankruptcy, losing her home and finding herself deeply in debt. She was unable to pay hospital bills for her mother, and she was now unemployed.

I explained to this woman the magic formula of changing water into wine. Again we made it clear to her that *wine* means answered prayer or the objectification of her ideal.

She was quarreling with the outside world. She said, "Look at the facts: I have lost everything; it is a cruel world. I cannot pay my bills. I do not pray; for I have lost hope." She was so absorbed and engrossed in the material world that she was completely oblivious to the internal cause of her situation. As we talked, she began to understand that she had to resolve the quarrel in her mind.

No matter what your desire or ideal is as you read this book, you will also find some thought or idea in your mind opposed to it. For example, your desire may be for health; perhaps there are several thoughts such as these in your mind simultaneously: "I can't be healed. I have tried, but it is no use; it's getting worse." "I don't know enough about spiritual mind healing,"

As you study yourself, don't you have a tug of war in your mind? Like this girl, you find environment and external affairs challenging your desire of expression, wealth, and peace of mind.

True prayer is a mental marriage feast, and it teaches us all how to resolve the mental conflict. In prayer you "write" what you *believe* in your own mind. Emerson said, "A man is what he thinks all day long." By your habitual thinking you make your own mental laws of belief. By repeating a certain train of thought you establish definite opinions and beliefs in the deeper mind called the subconscious; then such mental acceptances, beliefs, and opinions direct and control all the outer actions. To understand this and begin to apply it is the first step in changing "water into wine," or changing lack and limitation into abundance and opulence. The man who is unaware of his own inner, spiritual powers is, therefore, subject to race beliefs, lack, and limitation.

Open your Bible now, and perform your first miracle,

as this hair salon operator did. You can do it. If you merely read the Bible as a historical event, you will miss the spiritual, mental, scientific view of the laws of mind with which we are concerned in this book.

Let us take this passage: "And the third day there was a marriage in Cana of Galilea; and the mother of Jesus was there." *Galilee* means your mind or consciousness. *Cana* means your desire. The *marriage* is purely mental or the subjective embodiment of your desire. This whole, beautiful drama of prayer is a psychological one in which all the characters are mental states, feelings, and ideas within you.

One of the meanings of *Jesus* is illumined reason. The *mother of Jesus* means the feeling, moods, or emotions which possess us.

"And both Jesus was called, and his disciples, to the marriage." *Your disciples* are your inner powers and faculties enabling you to realize your desires.

"And when they wanted wine, the mother of Jesus saith unto him, They have no wine." *Wine,* as we have stated, represents the answered prayer or the manifestation of your desire and ideals in life. You can now see this is an everyday drama taking place in your own life.

When you wish to accomplish something as this girl did, namely, finding work, supply, and a way out of your problem, suggestions of lack come to you, such as, "There is no hope. All is lose. I can't accomplish it; it is hopeless." This is the voice from the outside world saying to you, "They have no wine" or "Look at the facts." This is your feeling of lack, limitation, or bondage speaking.

How do you meet the challenge of circumstances and conditions? By now you are getting acquainted with the laws of mind which are as follows: "As I think and feel inside, so is my outside world; i.e., my body, finances, environment, social position, and all phases of my external relationship to the world and man. Your internal, mental movements and imagery govern, control, and direct the external plane in your life.

The Bible says, "As he thinketh in his heart, so *is* he." The *heart* is a Chaldean word meaning the subconscious mind. In other words your thought must reach subjective levels by engaging the power of your subliminal self.

Thought and feeling are your destiny. Thought charged with feeling and interest is always subjectified, and becomes manifest in your world. *Prayer* is a marriage of thought and feeling, or your idea and emotion; this is what the marriage feast relates.

Any idea or desire of the mind felt as true comes to pass, whether it is good, bad, or indifferent. Knowing the law now that what you imagine and feel in your mind, you will express, manifest, or experience in the outside, enables you to begin to discipline your mind.

When the suggestion of lack, fear, doubt, or despair (they have no wine) comes to your mind, immediately reject it mentally by focusing your attention at once on the answered prayer, or the fulfillment of your desire.

The statement given in the Bible from John 2, "Mine hour is not yet come," and "Woman, what have I to do with thee," are figurative, idiomatic, oriental expressions.

As we paraphrase the quotation, *woman* means the negative feeling that you indulge in. These negative suggestions have no power of reality, because there is nothing to back them up.

A suggestion of lack has no power; the power is resident in your own thought and feeling.

What does God mean to you? *God* is the Name given to the One Spiritual Power. *God* is the One Invisible Source from which all things flow.

When your thoughts are constructive and harmonious, the spiritual power being responsive to your thought flows as harmony, health, and abundance. Practice the wonderful discipline of completely rejecting every thought of lack by immediately recognizing the availability of the spiritual power, and its response to your constructive thoughts and imagery; then you will be practicing the truth found in these words, "Woman what have I to do with thee?"

We read, "Mine hour is not yet come." This means that while you have not yet reached a conviction or positive state of mind, you know you are on the way mentally, because you are engaging your mind on the positive ideals, goals, and objectives in life. Whatever the mind dwells upon, it multiplies, magnifies, and causes it to grow until finally the mind becomes qualified with the new state of consciousness. You are then conditioned positively, whereas before you were conditioned negatively.

The spiritual man in prayer moves from the mood of lack to the mood of confidence, peace, and trust in the spiritual power within himself. Since his trust and faith are in the Spiritual Power, his mother (mood and feeling) registers a feeling of triumph or victory; this will bring about the solution or the answer to your prayer.

The waterpots in the story from the Bible refer to the mental cycles that man goes through in order to bring about the subjective realization of his desire. The length of time may be a moment, hour, week, or month depending on the faith and state of consciousness of the student.

In prayer we must cleanse our mind of false beliefs, fear, doubt, and anxiety by becoming completely detached from the evidence of senses and the external world. In the peacefulness and quietude of your mind, wherein you have stilled the wheels of your mind, meditate on the joy of the answered prayer until that inner certitude comes, whereby *you know that you know.* When you have succeeded in being *one* with your desire, you have succeeded in the mental marriage—or the union of your feeling with your idea.

I am sure you wish to be married (one with) to health, harmony, success, and achievement in your mind at this moment. Every time you pray you are trying to perform the *marriage feast of Cana* (realization of your desire or ideas). You want to be mentally identified with the concept of peace, success, well-being, and perfect health.

"They filled them up to the brim." *The six waterpots* represent your own mind in the spiritual and mental creative act. You must fill your mind *to the brim,* meaning you must become filled full of the feeling of being what you long to be. When you succeed in filling your mind with the ideal you wish to accomplish or express, you are full to the brim; then you cease praying about it; for you feel its reality in your mind. You *know!* It is a finished state of consciousness. You are at peace about it.

"And he saith unto them, Draw out now, and bear unto the governor of the feast." Whatever is impregnated in our subsconscious mind is always objectified on the screen of space; consequently when we enter a state of conviction that our prayer is answered, we have given the command, "Bear unto the governor of the feast."

You are always governing your mental feast. During the day thousands of thoughts, suggestions, opinions, sights, and sounds reach your eyes and ears. You can reject them as unfit for mental consumption or entertain them as you choose. Your conscious, reasoning, intellectual mind is the governor of the feast. When you consciously choose to entertain, meditate, feast upon, and imagine your heart's desire as true, it becomes a living embodiment, and a part of your mentality, so that your deeper self gives birth or expression to it. In other words what is impressed subjectively is expressed objectively. Your senses or conscious mind sees the objectification of your good. When the conscious mind becomes aware of "water made into wine," it becomes aware of the answered prayer. *Water* might be called, also, the invisible, formless, spiritual power, unconditioned consciousness. *Wine* is conditioned consciousness, or the mind giving birth to its beliefs and convictions.

The servants which draw the water for you represent the mood of peace, confidence, and faith. According to your faith or feeling, your good is attracted or drawn to you.

Imbibe, cherish, fall in love with these spiritual principles which are discussed in this book. In the first recorded miracle of Jesus, you are told that prayer is a marriage feast, or the mind uniting with its desire.

Love is the fulfilling of the law. Love is really an emotional attachment, a sense of oneness with your good. You must be true to that which you love. You must be loyal to your purpose or to your ideal. We are not being true to the one we love, when we are flirting or mentally entertaining other marriages with fear, doubt, worry, anxiety, or false beliefs. Love is a state of oneness, a state of fulfillment. (Refer to the book by the author, *Love Is Freedom*.)

When this simple drama was explained to the hair salon operator mentioned above, she became rich mentally. She understood this drama, and she put it into practice in her life. This is how she prayed: She knew that the *water* (her own mind) would flow, and fill up all the *empty vessels* in response to her new way of thinking and feeling.

At night this client became very quiet and still, relaxed her body, and began to use constructive imagery. The steps she used are as follows:

First step: She began to imagine the local bank manager was congratulating her on her wonderful deposits in the bank. She kept imagining that for about five minutes.

The second step: In her imagination she heard her mother saying to her, "I am so happy about your wonderful, new position." She continued to hear her say this in a happy, joyous way for about three to five minutes.

The third step: Vividly she imagined the writer was in front of her performing her marriage ceremony. This woman heard me saying as the officiating minister, "I now pronounce you man and wife." Completing this routine, she went off to sleep feeling filled full, i.e., sensing and feeling within herself the joy of the answered prayer.

Nothing happened for three weeks; in fact things got much worse, but she persevered, refusing to take "No" for her answer. She knew that in order to grow spiritually, she too had to perform her first miracle by changing her fear to faith, her mood of lack to a mood of opulence and prosperity, by changing consciousness (water) into the conditions, circumstances, and experiences she wished to express.

Consciousness, Awareness, Beingness, Principle, Spirit, or whatever Name you give It is the cause of all; it is the only Presence and Power. The Spiritual Power or Spirit within us is the cause and substance of all things. All things—birds, trees, stars, sun, moon, earth, gold, silver, and platinum—are its manifestations. It is the cause and substance of all things. "There is none else."

Understanding this she knew that *water* (consciousness) could become supply in the form of money, true place, or true expression for herself, health for her mother, as well as companionship and fullness of life. She saw this simple—yet profound—truth in the twinkling of an eye, and said to me, "I *accept* my good."

She knew that nothing is hidden from us; all of God is within us, waiting for our discovery and inquiry.

In less than a month this young girl got married. The writer performed the ceremony. I pronounced the words she heard me say over and over again in her meditative, relaxed state: "I now pronounce you man and wife!"

Her husband gave her a check for $24,000 as a wedding present, as well as a trip around the world. Her new expression as a hair salon operator was to beautify her home and garden, and make the desert of her mind rejoice and blossom as the rose.

She changed "water into wine." *Water*, or her consciousness, became charged or conditioned by her constant, true, happy imagery. These images, when sustained regularly, systematically, and with faith in the developing powers of the deeper mind, will come out of the darkness (subconscious mind) into light (objectified on the screen of space.)

There is one important rule: Do not expose this newly developed film to the shattering light of fear, doubt, despondency, and worry. Whenever worry or fear knocks at your door, immediately turn to the picture you developed in your mind, and say to yourself, "A beautiful picture is being developed now in the dark house of my mind." Mentally pour on that picture your feeling of joy, faith, and understanding. You know you have operated a psychological, spiritual law; for what is impressed shall be expressed. It is wonderful!

The following is a sure, certain way for developing and manifesting all the material riches and supply you need all the days of your life. If you apply this formula sincerely and honestly, you should be amply rewarded on the external plane. I will illustrate this by telling you of a man who came to see me in London in desperate financial straits. He was a member of the Church of England, and had studied the working of the subconscious mind to some extent.

I told him to say frequently during the day, "God is the source of my supply, and all my needs are met at every moment of time and point of space." Think also of all the animal life in this world, and in all the galaxies of space which are now being taken care of by an Infinite Intelligence. Notice how nature is lavish, extravagant, and bountiful. Think of the fish of the sea which are all being sustained, as well as the birds of the air!"

He began to realize that since he was born, he had been taken care of; fed by his mother; clothed by his father, and watched over by tender, loving parents. This man got a job and was paid in a wonderful way. He reasoned that it was illogical to assume that the Principle of Life which gave him life, and always took care of him would suddenly cease to respond to him.

He realized that he had cut off his own supply by resenting his employer, self-condemnation, criticism of himself, and by his own sense of unworthiness. He had psychologically severed the cord which joined him to the Infinite Source of all things—the Indwelling Spirit or Life Principle, called by some "Consciousness or Awareness."

Man is not fed like the birds; he must consciously commune with the Indwelling Power and Presence, and receive guidance, strength, vitality, and all things necessary for the fulfillment of his needs.

This is the formula which he used to change water into the wine of abundance and financial success. He realized God or the Spiritual Power within him was the cause of all; furthermore he realized that if he could sell himself the idea that wealth was his by Divine right, he would manifest abundance of supply.

The affirmation he used was, "God is the source of my supply. All my financial and other needs are met at every moment of time and point of space; there is always a divine surplus." This simple statement repeated frequently, knowingly, and intelligently conditioned his mind to a prosperity consciousness.

All he had to do was to sell himself this positive idea, in the same way a good salesman has to sell himself on the merits of his product. Such a person is convinced of the integrity of his company, the high quality of the product, the good service which it will give the customer, and the fact that the price is right, etc.

I told him whenever negative thoughts came to his mind, which would happen, not to fight them, quarrel with them in any way, but simply go back to the spiritual, mental formula, and repeat it quietly and lovingly to himself. Negative thoughts came to him in avalanches at times in the form of a flood of negativity. Each time he met them with the positive, firm, loyal conviction: "God supplies all my needs; there is a Divine surplus in my life."

He said as he drove his car, and went through his day's routine, that a host of sundry, miscellaneous, negative concepts crowded his mind from time to time; such as, "There is no hope." "You are broke." Each time such negative thoughts came, he refused their mental admission by turning to the Eternal Source of wealth, health, and all things which he knew to be his own spiritual awareness. Definitely and positively he claimed, "God is the source of my supply, and that supply is mine now!" Or, "There is a Divine solution. God's wealth is my wealth," and other affirmative, positive statements which charged his mind with hope, faith, expectancy, and ultimately a conviction in an ever-flowing fountain of riches supplying all his needs copiously, joyously, and endlessly.

The negative flood of thoughts came to him as often as fifty times in an hour; each time he refused to open the door of his mind to these gangsters, assassins, and thieves which he knew would only rob him of peace, wealth, success, and all good things. Instead he opened the door of his mind to the idea of God's Eternal Life Principle of supply flowing through him as wealth, health, energy, power, and all things necessary to lead a full and happy life here.

As he continued to do this, the second day not so many

thieves knocked at his door; the third day, the flow of negative visitors was less; the fourth day, they came intermittently, hoping for admission, but receiving the same mental response: "No entrance! I accept only thoughts and concepts which activate, heal, bless, and inspire my mind!"

He reconditioned his consciousness or mind to a wealth consciousness. "The prince of this world cometh, and hath nothing in me"—This conveys to your mind: The negative thoughts, such as fear, lack, worry, anxiety came, but they received no response from his mind. He was now immune, God intoxicated, and seized by a divine faith in an ever-expanding consciousness of abundance and financial supply. This man did not lose everything; neither did he go into bankruptcy; he was given extended credit; his business improved; new doors opened up, and he prospered.

Remember always in the prayer-process, you must be loyal to your ideal, purpose, and objective. Many people fail to realize wealth and financial success because they pray two ways. They affirm God is their supply, and that they are divinely prospered, but a few minutes later they deny their good by saying, "I can't pay this bill." "I can't afford this, that, or the other things." Or they say to themselves, "A jinx is following me." "I can't ever make ends meet." "I never have enough to go around." All such statements are highly destructive, and neutralize your positive prayers. This is what is called "praying two ways."

You must be faithful to your plan or your goal. You

must be true to your knowledge of the spiritual power. Cease making negative marriages, i.e., uniting with negative thoughts, fears, and worries.

Prayer is like a captain directing the course of his ship. You must have a destination. You must know where you are going. The captain of the ship, knowing the laws of navigation, regulates his course accordingly. If the ship is turned from its course by storms or unruly waves, he calmly redirects it along its true course.

You are the captain on the bridge, and you are giving the orders in the way of thoughts, feelings, opinions, beliefs, moods, and mental tones. Keep your eye on the beam. *You go where your vision is!* Cease, therefore, looking at all the obstacles, delays, and impediments that would cause you to go off your course. Be definite and positive. Decide where you are going. Know that your mental attitude is the ship which will take you from the mood of lack and limitation, to the mood and feeling of opulence, and to the belief in the inevitable law of God working for you.

Quimby, who was a doctor, a wonderful student, and teacher of the mental and spiritual laws of mind, said, "Man acts as he is acted upon." What moves you now? What is it that determines your response to life? The answer is as follows: Your ideas, beliefs, and opinions activate your mind and condition you to the point that you become, as Quimby stated, "an expression of your beliefs." This illustrates the truth of Quimby's statement: "Man is belief expressed."

Another popular statement of Quimby's was, "Our minds mingle like atmospheres, and each person has his identity in that atmosphere." When you were a child, you were subject to the moods, feelings, beliefs, and the general, mental atmosphere of the home. The fears, anxieties, superstitions, as well as the religious faith and convictions of the parents were impressed on your mind.

Let us say the child had been brought up in a poverty-stricken home, in which there was never enough to go around, financially speaking; he heard constantly the complaint of lack and limitation.

You could say, like Salter in his conditioned-reflex therapy, that the child was conditioned to poverty. The young man may have a poverty complex based on his early experiences, training, and beliefs, but he can rise above any situation, and become free; this is done through the power of prayer.

I knew a young boy aged 17, who was born in a place called "Hell's Kitchen" in New York. He listened to some lectures I was giving in Steinway Hall, New York, at the time. This boy realized that he had been the victim of negative, destructive thinking, and that if he did not redirect his mind along constructive channels, the world-mind with its fears, failures, hates, and jealousies would move in and control him. "Man acts as he is acted upon."

It stands to reason, as Quimby knew, that if man will not take charge of his own house (mind), the propaganda, false beliefs, fears, and worries of the phenomenalistic world will act as a hypnotic spell over him.

We are immersed in the race mind which believes in sickness, death, misfortune, accident, failures, disease, and diverse disasters. Follow the Biblical injunction: "Come out from among them, and be separate." Identify yourself mentally and emotionally with the Eternal Verities which have stood the test of time.

This young man decided to think and plan for himself. He decided to take the Royal Road to Riches by accepting God's abundance here and now, and to fill his mind with spiritual concepts and perceptions. He knew, as he did this, he would automatically crowd out of his mind all negative patterns.

He adopted a simple process called "scientific imagination." He had a wonderful voice, but it was not cultivated or developed. I told him the image he gave attention to in his mind would be developed in his deeper mind and come to pass. He understood this to be a law of mind—a law of action and reaction—i.e., the response of the deeper mind to the mental picture held in the conscious mind.

This young man would sit down quietly in his room at home; relax his whole body, and vividly imagine himself singing before a microphone. He would actually reach out for the "feel" of the instrument. He would hear me congratulate him on his wonderful contract, and tell him how magnificent his voice was. By giving his attention and devotion to this mental image regularly and systematically, a deep impression was made on his subconscious mind.

A short time elapsed, and an Italian voice instructor in New York gave him free lessons several times a week, because he saw his possibilities. He got a contract which sent him abroad to sing in the salons of Europe, Asia, South Africa, and other places. His financial worries were over, for he also received a wonderful salary. His hidden talents and ability to release them were his real riches. These talents and powers within all of us are God-given; let us release them.

Did you ever say to yourself, "How can I be more useful to my fellow creature?" "How can I contribute more to humanity?"

A minister-friend of mine told me that in his early days he and his church suffered financially. His technique or process was this simple prayer which worked wonders for him: "God reveals to me better ways to present the truths of God to my fellow creature." Money poured in; the mortgage was paid in a few years, and he has never worried about money since.

As you read this chapter, you have now learned that the inner feelings, moods, and beliefs of man always control and govern his external world. The inner movement of the mind controls the outer movements. To change the outside, you must change the inside. "As in Heaven, so on earth"; or as in my mind or consciousness, so is it in my body, circumstances, and environment.

The Bible says, "There is nothing hidden that shall not be revealed." For example, if you are sick, you are revealing a mental and emotional pattern which is the cause. If you are upset, or if you receive tragic news, notice how you reveal it in your face, eyes, gestures, tonal qualities, also in your gait and posture. As a matter of fact your whole body reveals your inner distress. You could, of course, through mental discipline and prayer remain absolutely poised, serene, and calm, refusing to betray your hidden feelings or mental states. You could order the muscles of your body to relax, be quiet, and be still; they would have to obey you. Your eyes, face, and lips would not betray any sign of grief, anger, or despondency. On the other hand, with a little discipline, through prayer and meditation, you could reverse the entire picture. Even though you had received disturbing news, regardless of its grave nature, you could show and exhibit joy, peace, relaxation, and a vibrant, buoyant nature. No one would ever know that you were the recipient of so-called bad news.

Regardless of what kind of news you received today, you could go to the mirror, look at your face, lips, eyes, and your gestures, as you tell yourself, and imagine you have heard the news of having received a vast fortune. Dramatize it, feel it, thrill to it, and notice how your whole body responds to the inner thrill.

You can reverse any situation through prayer. Busy your mind with the concepts of peace, success, wealth, and happiness. Identify yourself with these ideas mentally, emotionally, and pictorially.

Get a picture of yourself as you want to be; retain that image; sustain it with joy, faith, and expectancy; finally you will succeed in experiencing its manifestation.

I say to people who consult me regarding financial lack to "marry wealth." Some see the point, others do not. As all Bible students know, your *wife* is what you are mentally joined to, united with, or at one with.

In other words, what you conceive and believe, you give it conception. If you believe the world is cold, cruel, and harsh, that it is a "dog eat dog" way of life, that is *your* concept; you are married to it, and you will have children or issue by that marriage. The children from such a mental marriage or belief will be your experiences, conditions, and circumstances together with all other events in your life. All your experiences and reactions to life will be the image and likeness of the ideas which fathered them.

Look at the many wives the average man is living with, such as fear, doubt, anxiety, criticism, jealousy, and anger; these play havoc with his mind. Marry wealth by claiming, feeling, and believing: "God supplies all my needs according to his riches in glory." Or take the following statement, and repeat it over and over again knowingly until your consciousness is conditioned by it, or it becomes a part of your meditation: "I am divinely expressed, and I have a wonderful income." Do not say this in a parrot-like fashion, but know that your train of thought is being engraved in your deeper mind, and it becomes a conditioned state of consciousness. Let the phrase become meaningful to you. Pour life, love, and feeling on it, making it alive.

One of my class-students recently opened a restaurant.

He phoned me saying that he got married to a restaurant; he meant that he had made up his mind to be very successful, diligent, and persevering, and to see that his business prospered. This man's *wife* (mental) was his belief in the accomplishment of his desire or wish.

Identify yourself with your aim in life, and cease mental marriages with criticism, self-condemnation, anger, fear, and worry. Give attention to your chosen ideal, being full of faith and confidence in the inevitable law of prosperity and success. You will accomplish nothing by loving your ideal one minute, and denying it the next minute; this is like mixing acid and an alkali; for you will get an inert substance. In going along the Royal Road to Riches, you must be faithful to your chosen ideal (your wife).

We find illustrations in the Bible relating to these same truths. For instance, "Eve came out of Adam's rib." *Your rib* is your concept, desire, idea, plan, goal, or aim in life.

Eve means the emotion, feeling nature, or the inner tone. In other words, you must mother the idea. The idea must be mothered, loved, and felt as true, in order to manifest your aim in life.

The *idea* is the father; the *emotion* is the mother; this is the marriage feast which is always taking place in your mind.

Ouspensky spoke of the third element which entered in or was formed following the union of your desire and feeling. He called it the neutral element. We may call it "peace"; for God is Peace.

The Bible says, "And the government shall be on his shoulders." In other words, let Divine Wisdom be your guide. Let the subjective Wisdom within you lead, guide, and govern you in all your ways. Turn over your request to this Indwelling Presence knowing in your heart and soul that it will dissipate the anxiety, heal the wound, and restore your soul to equanimity and tranquility. Open your mind and heart, and say, "God is my pilot. He leads me. He prospers me. He is my counsellor." Let your prayer be night and morning, "I am a channel through which God's riches flow ceaselessly, copiously, and freely." Write that prayer in your heart, inscribe it in your mind. Keep on the beam of God's glory!

The man who does not know the inner workings of his own mind is full of burdens, anxieties, and worries; for he has not learned how to cast his burden on the Indwelling Presence, and go free.

The Zen monk was asked by his disciple, "What is Truth?" He replied in a symbolic way by taking the bag off his back, and placing it on the ground.

The disciple then asked him, "Master, how does it work?"

The Zen monk still silent, placed the bag on his back, and walked on down the road singing to himself. The *bag* is your burden, or your problem. You cast it on the subjective Wisdom which knows all, and has the "know how" of accomplishment. It knows only the answer.

Placing the bag again on his back means though I still have the problem, I now have mental rest and relief from the burden, because I have invoked the Divine Wisdom on my behalf; therefore I sing the song of triumph, knowing that the answer to my prayer is on the way, and I sing for the joy that is set before me. It is wonderful.

"Every man at the beginning doth set forth good wine; and when men have well drunk, then that which is worse; but thou hast kept the good wine until now." This is true of every man when he first enters a knowledge of the laws of mind. He sets out with high spirits and ambitions. He is the new broom which sweeps clean, and he is full of good intentions; oftentimes he forgets the Source of power. He does not remain faithful to the Principle within him, which is scientific and effectual, that would lift him out of his negative experiences, and set him on the high road to freedom and peace of mind. He begins to indulge mentally and emotionally with ideas and thoughts extraneous to his announced aim and goal. In other words he is not faithful to his ideal or wife.

Know that the subjective or deep self within you will accept your request, and being the great fabricator, it will bring it to pass in its own way. All you do is release your request with faith and confidence, in the same way you would cast a seed on the ground, or mail a letter to a friend, knowing the answer would come.

Did you ever go between two great rocks and listen to the echo of your voice? This is the way the Life Principle within you answers. *You* will hear the echo of your own voice. Your *voice* is your inner, mental movement of the mind—your inner, psychological journey where you feasted mentally on an idea until you were full; then you rested.

Knowing this law and how to use it, be sure you never become drunk with power, arrogance, pride, or conceit. Use the law to bless, heal, inspire, and lift up others, as well as yourself.

Man misuses the law by selfishly taking advantage of his fellow man; if you do, you hurt and attract loss to yourself. Power, security, and riches are not to be obtained externally. They come from the treasure-house of eternity within. We should realize that the *good wine* is always present, for God is the Eternal Now. Regardless of present circumstances, you can prove your good is ever-present by detaching yourself mentally from the problem, going on the High Watch, and go about your Father's business.

To go on the High Watch is to envision your good, to dwell on the new concept of yourself, to become married to it, and sustain the happy mood by remaining faithful—full of faith every step of the way—knowing that the wine of joy, the answered prayer, is on the way. "Now is the day of salvation." "The kingdom of heaven is at hand." "Thou hast kept the good wine until now."

You can—this moment—travel psychologically in your mind, and enter mentally through divine imagination into any desired state. The wealth, health, or invention you wish to introduce are all invisible first. Everything comes out of the Invisible. You must subjectively process riches, before you can objectively possess wealth. The feeling of wealth produces wealth; for wealth is a state of consciousness. *A state of consciousness* is how you think, feel, believe, and what you mentally give consent to.

A teacher in California receiving over five or six thousand dollars a year looked in a window at a beautiful ermine coat that was priced at $8,000. She said, "It would take me years to save that amount of money. I could never afford it. Oh, how I want it!" She listened to our lectures on Sunday mornings. By ceasing to marry these negative concepts, she learned that she could have a coat, car, or anything she wished without hurting anybody on the face of the earth.

I told her to imagine she had the coat on, to feel its beautiful fur, and to get the feel of it on her. She began to use the power of her imagination prior to sleep at night. She put the imaginary coat on her, fondled it, caressed it, like a child does with her doll. She continued to do this, and finally felt the thrill of it all.

She went to sleep every night wearing this imaginary coat, and being so happy in possessing it. Three months went by, and nothing happened. She was about to waver, but she reminded herself that it is the sustained mood, which demonstrates. "He who perseveres to the end shall be saved." The solution will come to the person who does not waver, but always goes about with the perfume of His Presence with him. The answer comes to the man who walks in the light that "It is done!" You are always using the *perfume of His Presence* when you sustain the happy, joyous mood of expectancy knowing your good is on the way. You saw it on the unseen, and you *know* you will see it in the seen.

The sequel to the teacher's drama of the mind is interesting. One Sunday morning after our lecture, a man accidentally stepped on her toe, apologized profusely, asked her where she lived, and offered to drive her home. She accepted gladly. Shortly after, he proposed marriage; gave her a beautiful diamond ring, and said to her, "I saw the most wonderful coat; you would simply look radiant wearing it!" It was the coat she admired three months previously. (The salesman said over one hundred wealthy women looked at the coat, admired it immensely, but for some reason always selected another garment.)

Through your capacity to choose, imagine the reality of what you have selected, and through faith and perseverance, *you can* realize your goal in life. All the riches of heaven are here now within you waiting to be released. Peace, joy, love, guidance, inspiration, goodwill, and abundance all exist now. All that is necessary in order to express God's riches is for you to leave the present now (your limitation), enter into the mental vision or picture, and in a happy, joyous mood become one with your ideal. Having seen and felt your good in moments of high exaltation, you know that in a little while you shall see your ideal objectively as you walk through time and space. As within, so without. As above, so below. As in heaven, so on earth. In other words, you will see your beliefs expressed. Man *is* belief expressed!

HOW SUCCESS GROWS *from* FAILURE

Napoleon Hill

Turn back the pages of history, back to the very beginning of all that we know of civilization, and you will find that the men and women whose names lived after they passed on were those whose efforts were born of struggle, hardship, and failure.

Men may leave behind them monuments of marble without struggle, hardship, and failure, but those who would build monuments in the hearts of their fellowmen, where neither the disintegrating forces of the elements nor the degrading hand of man can destroy them, must pay the price in sacrifice and struggle.

Ten years ago a baby was born into one of the wealthiest families in America. The whole world showered the little fellow with gifts it did not need and could not use. One foolish king sent, as his offering to the useless collection, a gold crib that cost $40,000.

I was going to law school in the city where that baby was born, therefore I know considerable about the event. That bountiful shower of gifts reminded me of the passage in the Bible that reads something along these lines: "To him that hath it shall be given, and to him that hath not it shall be taken away, even that which he hath."

Nothing more true to human nature was ever said than this. Like attracts like. Wealth attracts wealth and poverty attracts poverty. It is the way of human nature.

By and by, this little baby grew old enough to be taken on the streets. When he was taken out, he was flanked by a coterie of servants and private detectives whose business it was to see that no misfortune overtook him. Never in all this baby's life was he permitted outside the protecting influence of these servants. He could not go on the street alone. He was watched over with care that would lead one to believe he might have been made of superior clay.

This little fellow had no cares. He experienced no hardships. He never knew what struggle meant. All he knew was that he was not born to toil. He did not have to dress himself; he had servants for that purpose. He did not have to use his eyes; he had servants' eyes to use. He did not have to use his hands; he had servants' hands to use. In fact he did not have to do anything.

Each winter he went with his army of servants to play in the rolling waters of the warm Gulf of Mexico, where he was not bothered with the cold blizzards of the north. When he went out to swim he was surrounded by this same army of servants, who flanked him and watched to see that no harm befell him.

Two years ago this little fellow, now a boy of ten years, had just returned to the north from his wintering place in Florida. He was out in the gardens with his servants when he noticed that the gates were open, and he saw beyond the much longed-for freedom that every normal child is constantly seeking. While the servants' vigilance had slackened for a moment, he saw his chance and made a run for the street. He got outside and into the middle of the street when he was run down and instantly killed by a Ford automobile.

At the very moment this was happening, there were no less than a million little urchins located in the crowded streets of the great cities, not one of which could have been run down by an automobile in an open ten-acre field, because these little "unfortunates" had learned the art of self-defense. Out of struggle—struggle born of necessity—they had learned to get out of the way of automobiles.

Verily do we repeat that out of struggle and hardship come endurance and power!

Servants and private detectives can watch over a baby and possibly keep him from being stolen; they can even keep him from being run down by automobiles, if they attend to their duties properly, but the eternal law of compensation takes its toll when the little fellow grows up to maturity and commences to take his place among men. He pays dearly for the early protection that relieved him of struggle the very first time he is called upon to rely entirely on his own resources, because he finds that he has no real "resources."

The strong-armed blacksmith developed his strength out of "resistance." The greater the resistance, the greater his strength. By wielding a heavy hammer day in and day out, he finally grew a mighty arm that serves him wherever physical strength is needed. He developed his strong arm in exactly the same manner that all strength must be developed: by overcoming resistance.

We point with pride to Lincoln as being one of the really great Americans of the past, yet how many stop to consider that his strength, both physical and moral, grew out of hardship and struggle! No doubt Nancy Hanks would have given Lincoln as royal a birth as that of the little boy mentioned above, if she had been financially able, but if she had done so there is but little doubt that Lincoln would never have risen to the heights to which he attained!

Much of Lincoln's greatness grew out of his early struggles and hardships, because out of these grew strength, that mighty strength which carried him through one of the most trying crises of this country.

The most dangerous handicap with which any child could be surrounded is the handicap of money, provided it is used to relieve the child of struggle.

Twenty-odd years ago I was secretary to a wealthy man whose two sons were away at college. It was a part of my duty to make out a check for $100 for each of these boys on the first of the month. This was their "spending money," and spend it they did!

Well do I remember how I envied these boys the easy time this monthly remittance provided. By and by, they returned home with their "sheep skins" and other things too, among them being the capacity for great quantities of whiskey.

One of those boys is now under the sod and the other is in an insane asylum, a victim of "D.T.'s."

Last year I had the privilege of speaking in the college where one of the boys went to school. The principal of the school told me that the $100 check which came monthly for that boy was the influence that undermined him. With that check he had money to be a "good fellow." This led to the drink habit, and that led to ruination!

I can see now that fate dealt me a lucky blow when it placed the great cosmic urge of necessity behind me, in my early childhood, and forced me to struggle for a schooling and for existence itself. That struggle seemed hard then, but I know now that it was the strengthening process I needed to prepare me for a man's work in life.

My own boys are coming along now, and in spite of the powerful moral which I have drawn from my own experience and from my observation of the two boys mentioned, I see myself inclined to "make it easy" for my boys when I can. This is a common tendency—a human sort of tendency, perhaps—which can lead nowhere but to distress and grief when the child is called upon for the reserve strength that is not there because he has never met with the necessary resistance.

It may seem like a trite statement, but it is nonetheless true on that account, to say the only permanent good that can come to a child comes out of what he does for himself. The greatest service that can be rendered any person on earth is the service which causes that person to rely upon himself.

When you pitch a dime to a beggar you may benefit him temporarily, but in the long run you have done him a decided injury, because you have taken away from him the necessity of struggle.

I met a man in Lawton, Oklahoma, on my recent tour of the country, who gave me much food for thought. I had ridden around with him all afternoon in an automobile before I learned that he was stone blind. His dark glasses covered his eyes, and not a sign of his affliction was to be seen on his face or detected from his voice. He laughingly carried on one of the most interesting conversations I have ever listened to, and entertained me so splendidly that I did not notice his blindness.

Afterward I learned of this man's early struggles. He had lost his eyes at the age of four. Several years ago he presented himself at Northwestern University, in the city of Chicago, for matriculation as a student. The officials refused to accept him, urging him not to undertake a stiff course such as tried the strength of able-bodied young men and women to the utmost.

But this young fellow knew no defeat! He was persistent. Finally the university officials asked him how much money he had with which to pay his way through school, and he replied, "Thirty-five dollars."

They told him he would only be wasting his time to start in school with his handicap without sufficient funds, and advised him not to try it. He went out and walked around the block a time or two and then came back and said, "Now, look here. Let me enter for the first semester, and if I do not keep up with my classes and pay my way, you can turn me out." They consented, largely, I suspect, because they did not have the heart to refuse.

This young man not only completed the first semester with honors, at the head of his classes, but he finished the entire course—leading all the way through.

But this is not all. He paid his way by taking notes in the lecture rooms, transcribing them on the typewriter, and selling copies to his fellow students—those who had two perfectly good eyes and money in the bank besides!

Rarely does a person ever have opportunity to test the limits of his ability. We can accomplish pretty much whatever we make up our minds to accomplish. If we are not forced to test our strength through dire necessity, through struggle, through hardship, we seldom discover our possibilities. Lay it down as a general rule—and a sound one at that—that real strength comes from struggle, hardship, adversity, and handicaps imposed upon us by causes beyond our immediate control. If we could "control" these causes, they would not exist because we would eliminate them, thereby depriving ourselves of the most beneficial experience that can come to a human being.

Twenty-odd years ago I found myself forced to work as a laborer in the coal mines. Nothing short of necessity would have induced me to perform such work, yet out of that very work came experience that has played, and is now playing, no small part in the very best service I have rendered and will continue to render my fellowmen. We are in the midst of a great industrial crisis, not alone in America but throughout the world, and much of our effort is directed toward the elimination of the "cause" out of which this crisis grew. These efforts have not been without visible results, something that would not have been possible except for the "forced service" rendered in the coal mines years ago. This brought me close to the people who labor in those mines and gave me a splendid chance to study the conditions under which they work, the grievances of which they complain, their faults, and their virtues.

Now when I presume to write for or about those who perform the most lowly sort of labor, I write not as one whose hands were never covered with the grime and dust of honest toil, but as one who has worked shoulder to shoulder with these men whose voices are now crying out for justice and fair treatment.

And when I send back the message to the laborers out of whose ranks I came, urging them to "perform more work and better work than actually paid for," I know that I am not leading them astray or counseling them unwisely, because it has been this one practice, more than any other, that has helped me to throw off an undesirable, unprofitable environment and get into the work that I love. The reason why this is sound practice is obvious. It develops greater and greater ability until, finally, a man just naturally bursts out of his cramped environment by attracting the attention of men in a more desirable walk of life. Out of effort and resistance comes strength! The greater the effort, the greater the compensating strength, and the man who foolishly withholds the best service he is capable of rendering because he may not be receiving what it is worth, is only prolonging the time of failure.

I know of no other single quality that has paid me greater dividends and carried me further toward my ultimate goal in life than has the habit of performing more service and better service than was actually paid for!

But lay stress on that word *habit*.

This practice must become a habit, and recognition must be gained before the real results begin to show. To merely perform more service and better service than is paid for one day, and refrain from doing it the other five working days of the week, would be something like training one hour a week for a prize fight and resting the remainder of the time.

Out of resistance comes strength!

A man may be "born to the weary treadmill of toil," but if he understands that out of toil, out of resistance, out of effort, out of adversity comes strength, he will not long remain a victim of this handicap. Instead, he will soon burst the cords of circumstances and environment, no matter how strong they may seem, and rise to claim his own—his own that is born of struggle and hardship.

A TOAST TO THE MAN WHO FAILS!

As my fingers begin to play upon the keyboard of my typewriter, I look and see before me a great army of men whose faces show the lines of care and despair.

Some are in rags, having reached the last stage of that long, long trail which all men fight to avoid: failure!

Others are in better circumstances, but the fear of starvation shows plainly on their faces, the smile of courage has left their lips, and they, too, seem to have given up the fight.

The scene shifts. I look again and am carried backward into the events of history past, and there I see, also, the failures of the past—failures which have meant more to the human race than all the successes recorded in the history of the world.

I see the homely face of Socrates as he stood at the very end of that trail which men call failure, waiting, with upturned eyes, through those moments that must have seemed like an eternity, just before he drank the poisoned hemlock.

I see Christopher Columbus standing in a Spanish dungeon, a prisoner in chains, the tribute paid him for his sacrifice when he set sail on an unknown ocean to discover an unknown world, knowing that the chances were greatly in favor of his never returning to his native land.

I see the face of Thomas Paine, the man whom the English sought to capture and put to death as the real instigator of the American Revolution. I see him lying in a filthy prison in France, waiting calmly under the shadow of the guillotine, a reprieve from death, and writing—as he waited—many pages dedicated to the advancement of human liberty.

And I see, also, the face of the man from Galilee suffering on the cross at Calvary, the reward for his efforts to interest men in being decent with one another here on earth.

Failures, all!

Oh, to be such a failure. Oh, to go down in history, as these men did, as being brave enough to place humanity above the individual and principle above pecuniary gain. On such failures rest the hopes of the world.

THE TEST OF A MAN!

The measure of a real man is in his ability to see, with clear eyes, all the beauty and the good and all the injustice and the wrong there is in the world and still maintain an even sense of proportion in all things, toward all people.

I bow to the man who can see the imperfections of mankind without becoming cynical; who can temper justice with mercy; who can see the good there is in men who disagree with him; who can work in harmony with those whom he does not admire; who exercises self-control and lets reason instead of emotion govern his actions toward others.

Such a man was the immortal Lincoln!

He was a man with a message when he had sufficient provocation to have become a man with a grievance instead. As a reward for his greatness, the world has erected an everlasting monument to Lincoln's name. A monument that the elements can never disintegrate, that no depredating hand can destroy; a monument built in the heart of the people—built not of stone but of love, sympathy, patience, tolerance, and forgiveness for mankind— those gentle qualities that memory attaches to his name and which are now the real test of a man!

THE DAMAGING EFFECTS OF SUBTERFUGE AND DECEIT

Nothing really seems so very bad until someone tries to cover it up through subterfuge and deceit.

We may not agree with the man who boldly admits his shortcomings, but we cannot withhold from him a certain healthy respect on account of his boldness.

On the other hand, the moment a person resorts to secrecy or to subterfuge, even in connection with matters of small importance, that person becomes immediately marked as unworthy of trust.

If there is a skeleton in the closet which is apt to crawl

out to plague one at the most inopportune time, a mighty good plan is to voluntarily drag it out and say, "There it is; what are you going to do about it?"

People will forgive most anything unless there is an attempt to cover it up and clothe it in secrecy. In that event forgiveness comes reluctantly, if at all.

Many a solid friend has been made by open frankness in connection with matters that, within themselves, were of small importance, while on the other hand lifelong enemies have been made by lack of this frankness.

If a person is secretive and resorts to deceit and subterfuge in small matters, the supposition is that in matters of greater import the same tactics will prevail.

DELIVER MORE SERVICE AND BETTER SERVICE THAN YOU ARE PAID FOR

This simple injunction comes from a man who started at the very bottom, in the most lowly sort of labor.

It constitutes the keynote of almost every public address this man delivers; it permeates nearly everything he writes; it creeps into his everyday conversation.

There are many reasons why this is sound counsel, only one of which need be mentioned—namely, every person who forms the habit of delivering this sort of service soon attracts the attention of competitive bidders for his services. He stands out above the common crowd like a skyscraper above the ordinary buildings, and there is keen competition for his labor.

Give the best service you know how to render, regardless of the amount you receive for it, and soon—much sooner than you might imagine—you will become a "marked" person and greater responsibilities and higher wages will be thrusting themselves upon you.

Deliver the best services you can, not necessarily out of consideration for the purchaser but out of consideration for yourself! Failure to practice this habit is the chief obstacle that stands between 95 percent of the people and success, but of course this does not apply to you. Or does it?

Aimlessness is a sin and it leads straight to poverty, misery, want, and failure. A man without a definite, constructive purpose in life is simply one of nature's mistakes, because she did not intend to create such a being, in all probability.

SEVEN REMEDIES FOR A LEAN PURSE

George S. Clason

The glory of Babylon endures. Down through the ages its reputation comes to us as the richest of cities, its treasures as fabulous.

Yet it was not always so. The riches of Babylon were the results of the money wisdom of its people. They first had to learn how to become wealthy.

When the Good King, SARGON, returned to Babylon after defeating his enemies, the Elamites, he was confronted with a serious situation. The royal Chancellor explained it to the King thus:

"After many years of great prosperity brought to our people because your majesty built the great irrigation canals and the mighty temples to the Gods, now that these

Note to the Reader: The following story is a parable devised by Clason. His teaching method was to render financial advice in the form of mythical stories.

works are completed the people seem unable to support themselves.

"The laborers are without employment. The merchants have few customers. The farmers are unable to sell their produce. The people have not enough gold to buy food."

"But where has all the gold gone that we spent for these great improvements?" demanded the King.

"It has found its way, I fear," responded the Chancellor, "into the possession of a few very rich men of our city. It filtered through the fingers of most of our people as quickly as the goat's milk goes through the strainer. Now that the stream of gold has ceased to flow, most of our people have nothing to show for their earnings."

The King was thoughtful for some time. Then he asked, "Why should so few men be able to acquire all the gold?"

"Because they know how," replied the Chancellor. "One may not condemn a man for succeeding because he knows how. Neither may one with justice take away from a man what he has fairly earned, to give to men of less ability."

"But why," demanded the King, "should not all the people learn how to accumulate gold and therefore become themselves rich and prosperous?"

"Quite possible, your excellency. But who can teach them? Certainly not the priests, because they know naught of money making."

"Who knows best in all our city how to become wealthy, Chancellor?" asked the King.

"Thy question answers itself, your majesty. Who has amassed the greatest wealth in Babylon?"

"Well said, my able Chancellor. It is Arkad. He is the richest man in Babylon. Bring him before me on the morrow."

Upon the following day, as the King had decreed, Arkad appeared before him, straight and sprightly despite his three score years and ten.

"Arkad," spoke the King, "is it true thou art the richest man in Babylon?"

"So it is reported, your majesty, and no man disputes it."

"How becamest thou so wealthy?"

"By taking advantage of opportunities available to all citizens of our good city."

"Thou hadst nothing to start with?"

"Only a great desire for wealth. Besides this, nothing."

"Arkad," continued the King, "our city is in a very unhappy state because a few men know how to acquire wealth and therefore monopolize it, while the mass of our citizens lack the knowledge of how to keep any part of the gold they receive.

"It is my desire that Babylon be the wealthiest city in the world. Therefore, it must be a city of many wealthy men. Therefore, we must teach all the people how to acquire riches. Tell me, Arkad, is there any secret to acquiring wealth? Can it be taught?"

"It is practical, your majesty. That which one man knows can be taught to others."

The king's eyes glowed. "Arkad, thou speaketh the

words I wish to hear. Wilt thou lend thyself to this great cause? Wilt thou teach thy knowledge to a school for teachers, each of whom shall teach others until there are enough trained to teach these truths to every worthy subject in my domain?"

Arkad bowed and said, "I am thy humble servant to command. Whatever of knowledge I possess will I gladly give for the betterment of my fellowmen and the glory of my King. Let your good chancellor arrange for me a class of one hundred men and I will teach to them those Seven Remedies which did fatten my purse, than which there was none leaner in all Babylon."

A fortnight later, in compliance with the King's command, the chosen hundred assembled in the great hall of the Temple of Learning, seated upon colorful rugs in a semi-circle. Arkad sat beside a small taboret upon which smoked a sacred lamp sending forth a strange and pleasing odor.

"Behold the richest man in Babylon," whispered a student, nudging his neighbor as Arkad arose. "He is but a man even as the rest of us."

"As a dutiful subject of our great King," Arkad began, "I stand before you in his service. Because once I was a poor youth who did greatly desire gold, and because I found knowledge that enabled me to acquire it, he asks that I impart unto you my knowledge.

"I started my fortune in the humblest way. I had no advantage not enjoyed as fully by you and every citizen of Babylon.

"The first storehouse of my treasure was a well-worn purse. I loathed its useless emptiness. I desired that it be round and full, clinking with the sound of gold. Therefore, I sought every remedy for a lean purse. I found seven.

"To you, who are assembled before me, shall I explain the 'Seven Remedies for a Lean Purse' which I do recommend to all men who desire much gold. Each day for seven days will I explain to you one of the Seven Remedies.

"Listen attentively to the knowledge that I will impart. Debate it with me. Discuss it among yourselves. Learn these lessons thoroughly, that ye may also plant in your own purses the seed of wealth. First must each of you start wisely to build a fortune of his own. Then wilt thou be competent, and only then, to teach these truths to others.

"I shall teach to you in simple ways how to fatten your purses. This is the first step leading to the temple of wealth, and no man may climb who cannot plant his feet firmly upon the first step.

"We shall now consider the First Remedy."

THE FIRST REMEDY
Start thy purse to fattening

Arkad addressed a thoughtful man in the second row. "My good friend, at what craft workest thou?"

"I," replied the man, "am a scribe and carve records upon the clay tablets."

"Even at such labor did I myself earn my first coppers. Therefore, thou hast the same opportunity to build a fortune."

He spoke to a florid-faced man, farther back. "Pray tell also what dost thou to earn thy bread?"

"I," responded this man, "am a meat butcher. I do buy the goats the farmers raise and kill them and sell the meat to the housewives and the hides to the sandal makers."

"Because thou dost also labor and earn, thou hast every advantage to succeed that I did possess."

In this way did Arkad proceed to find out how each man labored to earn his living. When he had done questioning them, he said:

"Now, my students, ye can see that there are many trades and labors at which men may earn coins. Each of the ways of earning is a stream of gold from which the worker doth divert by his labors a portion to his own purse. Therefore into the purse of each of you flows a stream of coins large or small according to his ability. Is it not so?"

Thereupon they agreed that it was so.

"Then," continued Arkad, "if each of you desireth to build for himself a fortune, is it not wise to start by utilizing that source of wealth which he already has established?"

To this they agreed.

Then Arkad turned to a humble man who had declared himself an egg merchant. "If thou select one of thy baskets and put into it each morning ten eggs and take out from it each evening nine eggs, what will eventually happen?"

"It will become in time overflowing."

"Why?"

"Because each day I put in one more egg than I take out."

Arkad turned to the class with a smile. "Does any man here have a lean purse?"

First they looked amused. Then they laughed. Lastly they waved their purses in jest.

"All right," he continued, "now I shall tell thee the First Remedy I learned to cure a lean purse. Do exactly as I have suggested to the egg merchant. **For every ten coins thou placest within thy purse take out for use but nine. Thy purse will start to fatten at once and its increasing weight will feel good in thy hand and bring satisfaction to thy soul.**

"Deride not what I say because of its simplicity. Truth is always simple. I told thee I would tell how I built my fortune. This was my beginning. I, too, carried a lean purse and cursed it because there was naught within to satisfy my desires. But when I began to take out from my purse but nine parts of ten I put in, it began to fatten. So will thine.

"Now I will tell a strange truth, the reason for which I know not, when I ceased to pay out more than nine-tenths of my earnings, I managed to get along just as well. I was not shorter than before. Also, ere long, did coins come to me more easily than before. Surely it is a law of the Gods that unto him who keepeth and spendeth not a certain part of all his earnings, shall gold come more easily. Likewise, him whose purse is empty does gold avoid.

"Which desirest thou the most? Is it the gratification of thy desires of each day, a jewel, a bit of finery, better raiment, more food; things quickly gone and forgotten? Or is it substantial belongings, gold, lands, herds, merchandise, income bringing investments? The coins thou takest from thy purse bring the first. The coins thou leavest within it will bring the latter.

"This, my students, was the First Remedy I did discover for my lean purse: 'For each ten coins I put in, to spend but nine.' Debate this amongst yourselves. If any man proves it untrue, tell me upon the morrow when we shall meet again."

THE SECOND REMEDY
Control thy expenditures

"Some of your members, my students, have asked me this: 'How can a man keep one-tenth of all he earns in his purse when all the coins he earns are not enough for his necessary expenses?' " So did Arkad address his students upon the second day.

"Yesterday how many of thee carried lean purses?"

"All of us," answered the class.

"Yet, thou do not all earn the same. Some earn much more than others. Some have much larger families to support. Yet, all purses were equally lean. Now I will tell thee an unusual truth about men and sons of men. It is this: That what each of us calls our 'necessary expenses' will always grow to equal our incomes unless we protest to the contrary.

"**Confuse not thy necessary expenses with thy desires. Each of you, together with your good families, have more desires than your earnings can gratify.** Therefore, are thy earnings spent to gratify these desires insofar as they will go. Still thou retainest many ungratified desires.

"All men are burdened with more desires than they can gratify. Because of my wealth thinkest thou I may gratify every desire? 'Tis a false idea. There are limits to my time. There are limits to my strength. There are limits to the distance I may travel. There are limits to what I may eat. There are limits to the zest with which I may enjoy.

"I say to you that just as weeds grow in a field wherever the farmer leaves space for their roots, even so freely do desires grow in men whenever there is a possibility of their being gratified. **Thy desires are a multitude and those that thou mayest gratify are but few.**

"Study thoughtfully thy accustomed habits of living. Herein may be most often found certain accepted expenses that may wisely be reduced or eliminated. Let thy motto be one hundred per cent of appreciated value demanded for each coin spent.

"**Therefore, engrave upon the clay each thing for which thou desireth to spend. Select those that are necessary and others that are possible through the expenditure of nine-tenths of thy income.**

Cross out the rest and consider them but a part of that great multitude of desires that must go unsatisfied and regret them not.

"Budget then thy necessary expenses. Touch not the one-tenth that is fattening thy purse. Let this be thy great desire that is being fulfilled. Keep working with thy budget keep adjusting it to help thee. Make it thy first assistant in defending thy fattening purse."

Hereupon one of the students, wearing a robe of red and gold, arose and said, "I am a free man. I believe that it is my right to enjoy the good things of life. Therefore do I rebel against the slavery of a budget which determines just how much I may spend and for what. I feel it would take much pleasure from my life and make me little more than a pack-ass to carry a burden."

To him Arkad replied. "Who, my friend, would determine thy budget?"

"I would make it for myself," responded the protesting one.

"In that case were a pack-ass to budget his burden would he include therein jewels and rugs and heavy bars of gold? Not so. He would include hay and grain and a bag of water for the desert trail.

"The purpose of a budget is to help thy purse to fatten. It is to assist thee to have thy necessities and, insofar as attainable, thy other desires. It is to enable thee to realize thy most cherished desires by defending them from thy casual wishes. Like a bright light in a dark cave thy budget shows up the leaks from thy purse and enables thee to stop them and control thy expenditures for definite and gratifying purposes.

"This then is the Second Remedy for a lean purse. Budget thy expenses that thou mayest have coins to pay for thy necessities, to pay for thy enjoyments and to gratify thy worthwhile desires without spending more than nine-tenths of thy earnings."

THE THIRD REMEDY
Make thy gold multiply

"Behold thy lean purse is fattening. Thou hast disciplined thyself to leave therein one-tenth of all thou earneth. Thou hast controlled thy expenditures to protect thy growing treasure. Next, we will consider means to put thy treasure to labor and to increase. **Gold in a purse is gratifying to own and satisfieth a miserly soul but earns nothing. The gold we may retain from our earnings is but the start. The earnings it will make shall build our fortunes."** So spoke Arkad upon the third day to his class.

"How therefore may we put our gold to work? My first investment was unfortunate, for I lost all. Its tale I will relate later. My first profitable investment was a loan I made to a man named Aggar, a shield maker. Once each year did he buy large shipments of bronze brought from across the sea to use in his trade. Lacking sufficient capital to pay the merchants, he would borrow from those who had extra coins. He was an honorable man. His borrowing he would repay, together with a liberal rental, as he sold his shields.

"Each time I loaned to him I loaned back also the rental he had paid to me. Therefore not only did my capital increase, but its earning likewise increased. Most gratifying was it to have these sums return to my purse.

"I tell you, my students, a man's wealth is not in the coins he carries in his purse; it is the income he buildeth, the golden stream that continually floweth into his purse and keepeth it always bulging. That is what every man desireth. That is what thou, each one of thee desireth; an income that continueth to come whether thou work or travel.

"Great income I have acquired. So great that I am called a very rich man. My loans to Aggar were my first training in profitable investment. Gaining wisdom from this experience, I extended my loans and investments as my capital increased. From a few sources at first, from many sources later, flowed into my purse a golden stream of wealth available for such wise uses as I should decide.

"Behold, from my humble earnings I had begotten a hoard of golden slaves, each laboring and earning more gold. As they labored for me, so their children also labored and their children's children until great was the income from their combined efforts.

"Gold increaseth rapidly when making reasonable earnings as thou wilt see from the following: A farmer, when his first son was born, took ten pieces of silver to a money lender and asked him to keep it on rental for his son until he became twenty years of age. This the money lender did, and agreed the rental should be one-fourth of its value each four years. The farmer asked, because this sum he had set aside as belonging to his son, that the rental be added to the principal.

"When the boy had reached the age of twenty years, the farmer again went to the money lender to inquire about the silver. The money lender explained that because this sum had been increased by compound interest, the original ten pieces of silver had now grown to thirty and one-half pieces.

"The farmer was well pleased and because the son did not need the coins, he left them with the money lender. When the son became fifty years of age, the father meantime having passed to the other world, the money lender paid the son in settlement one hundred and sixty-seven pieces of silver.

"Thus in fifty years had the investment multiplied itself at rental almost seventeen times.

"This then is the Third Remedy for a lean purse, to put each coin to laboring that it may reproduce its kind even as the flocks of the field and help bring to thee income, a stream of wealth that shall flow constantly into thy purse."

THE FOURTH REMEDY
Guard thy treasures from loss

"Misfortune loves a shining mark. Gold in a man's purse must be guarded with firmness, else it be lost. Thus it is wise that we must first secure small amounts and learn to protect them before the Gods entrust us with larger." So spoke Arkad upon the fourth day to his class.

"Every owner of gold is tempted by opportunities whereby it would seem that he could make large sums by its investment in most plausible projects. Often friends and relatives are eagerly entering such investment and urge him to follow.

"The first sound principle of investment is security for thy principal. Is it wise to be intrigued by larger earnings when thy principal may be lost? I say not. The penalty of risk is probable loss. Study carefully before parting with thy treasure each assurance, that it may be safely reclaimed. Be not misled by thy own romantic desires to make wealth rapidly.

"Before thou loan it to any man assure thyself of his ability to repay and his reputation for doing so, that thou mayest not unwittingly be making him a present of thy hard earned treasure.

"Before thou entrust it as an investment in any field acquaint thyself with the dangers which may beset it.

"My own first investment was a tragedy to me at the time. The guarded savings of a year I did entrust to a brickmaker, named Azmur, who was traveling over the far seas and in Tyre agreed to buy for me the rare jewels of the Phoenicians. These we would sell upon his return and divide the profits. The Phoenicians were scoundrels and sold him bits of glass. My treasure was lost. Today, my training would show to me at once the folly of entrusting a brickmaker to buy jewels.

"Therefore, do I advise thee from the wisdom of my experiences: be not too confident of thy own wisdom in entrusting thy treasures to the possible pitfalls of investments. Better far consult the wisdom of those experienced is handling money for profit. Such advice is freely given for the asking and may readily possess a value equal in gold to the sum thou considerest investing. In truth such is its actual value, if it save thee from loss.

"This then is the Fourth Remedy for a lean purse, and of great importance if it prevent thy purse from being emptied once it has become well filled. **Guard thy treasure from loss by investing only where thy principal is safe, where it may be reclaimed if desirable, and where thou will not fail to collect a fair rental. Consult with wise men. Secure the advice of men experienced in the profitable handling of gold. Let their wisdom protect thy treasure from unsafe investment."**

THE FIFTH REMEDY
Make of thy dwelling a profitable investment

"If a man setteth aside nine parts of his earnings upon which to live and enjoy life, and if any part of this nine parts he can turn into a profitable investment without detriment to his well being, then so much faster will his treasures grow." So spake Arkad to his class at their fifth lesson.

"All too many of our men of Babylon do raise their families in unseemly quarters. They do pay to exacting landlords liberal rentals for rooms where their wives have not a spot to raise the blooms that gladden a woman's heart and their children have no place to play their games except in the unclean alleys.

"No man's family can fully enjoy life unless they do have a plot of ground wherein children can play in the clean earth and where the wife may raise not only blossoms but good rich herbs to feed her family.

"To a man's heart it brings gladness to eat the figs from his own trees and the grapes of his own vines. To own his own domicile and to have it a place he is proud to care for, putteth confidence in his heart and greater effort behind all his endeavors. Therefore, do I recommend that every man own the roof that sheltereth him and his.

"Nor is it beyond the ability of any well intentioned man to own his home. Hath not our great king so widely extended the walls of Babylon that within them much land is now unused and may be purchased at sums most reasonable?

"Also I say to you, my students, that the money lenders gladly consider the desires of men who seek homes and lands for their families. Readily may thou borrow to pay the brickmaker and the builder for such commendable purposes, if thou can show a reasonable portion of the necessary sum which thou thyself hath provided for the purpose.

"Then when the house be built, thou canst pay the money lender with the same regularity as thou didst pay the landlord. Because each payment will reduce thy indebtedness to the money lender, a few years will satisfy his loan.

"Then will thy heart be glad because thou wilt own in thy own right a valuable property and thy only cost will be the king's taxes.

"Also wilt thy good wife go more often to the river to wash thy robes, that each time returning she may bring a goatskin of water to pour upon the growing things.

"Thus come many blessings to the man who owneth his own house. And greatly will it reduce his cost of living, making available more of his earnings for pleasures and the gratification of his desires. This then is the Fifth Remedy for a lean purse. Own thy own home."

THE SIXTH REMEDY
Insure a future income

"The life of every man proceedeth from his childhood to his old age. This is the path of life and no man may deviate from it unless the Gods call him prematurely to the world beyond. **Therefore, do I say that it behooves a man to make preparation for a suitable income in the days to come, when he is no longer young and**

to make preparation for his family should he be no longer with them to comfort and support them. This lesson shall instruct thee in providing a full purse when time has made thee less able to earn." So Arkad addressed his class upon the sixth day.

"The man who because of his understanding of the laws of wealth, acquireth a growing surplus, should give thought to those future days. He should plan certain investments or provisions that may endure safely for many years, yet will be available when the time arrives which he has so wisely anticipated.

"There are diverse ways by which a man may provide with safety for his future. He may provide a hiding place and there bury a secret treasure. Yet, no matter with what skill it be hidden it may nevertheless become the loot of thieves. For this reason I recommend not this plan.

"A man may buy houses or lands for this purpose. If wisely chosen, as to their usefulness and value in the future they are permanent in their value and their earnings or their sale will provide well for his purpose.

"A man may loan a small sum to the money lender and increase it at regular periods. The rental which the money lender adds to this will largely add to its increase. I do know a sandal maker, named Ansan, who explained to me not long ago that each week for eight years he had deposited with his money lender two pieces of silver. The money lender had but recently given him an accounting over which he greatly rejoiced. The total of his small deposits with their rental at the customary rate of one-fourth their value for each four years, had now become a thousand and forty pieces of silver.

"I did gladly encourage him further by demonstrating to him with my knowledge of the numbers that in twelve years more, if he would keep his regular deposits of but two pieces of silver each week, the money lender would then owe him four thousand pieces of silver, a worthy competence for the rest of his life.

"Surely when such a small payment made with regularity doth produce such profitable results no man can afford not to insure a treasure for his old age and the protection of his family, no matter how prosperous his business and his investments may be.

"I would that I might say more about this. In my mind rests a belief that some day wise thinking men will devise a plan to insure men against death whereby many men pay in but a trifling sum regularly, the aggregate making a handsome sum for the family of each member who passeth to the beyond. This do I see as something desirable and which I could highly recommend. But today it is not possible because it must reach beyond the life of any man or any partnership to operate. It must be as stable as the King's throne. Some day do I feel that such a plan shall come to pass and be a great blessing to many men, because even the first small payment will make available a snug fortune for the family of a member should he pass on.

"But because we live in our own day and not in the days which are to come, must we take advantage of those means and ways of accomplishing our purposes. Therefore, do I recommend to all men, that they, by wise and well thought out methods, do provide against a lean purse in their mature years. For a lean purse to a man no longer able to earn or to a family without its head is a sore tragedy.

"This then is the Sixth Remedy for a Lean Purse. Provide in advance for the needs of thy growing age and the protection of thy family."

THE SEVENTH REMEDY
Increase thy ability to earn

"This day do I speak to thee, my students, of one of the most vital remedies for a lean purse. Yet, I will talk not of gold but of yourselves, of the men beneath the robes of many colors who do sit before me. I will talk to you of those things within the minds and lives of men which do work for or against their success." So did Arkad address his class upon the seventh day.

"Not long ago came to me a young man seeking to borrow. When I questioned him the cause of his necessity, he complained that his earnings were insufficient to pay his expenses. Thereupon I explained to him, this being the case, he was a poor customer for the money lender, as he possessed no surplus earning capacity to repay the loan.

" 'What you need, young man,' I told him, 'is to earn more coins. What dost thou to increase thy capacity to earn?'

" 'All that I can do,' he replied. 'Six times within two moons have I approached my master to request my pay be increased, but without success. No man can go oftener than that.'

"We may smile at his simplicity, yet he did possess one of the vital requirements to increase his earnings. Within him was a strong desire to earn more, a proper and commendable desire.

"Preceding accomplishment must be desire. Thy desires must be strong and definite. General desires are but weak longings. For a man to wish to be rich is of little purpose. For a man to desire five pieces of gold is a tangible desire which he can press to fulfillment. After he has backed his desire for five pieces of gold with strength of purpose to secure it, next he can find similar ways to obtain ten pieces and then twenty pieces and later a thousand pieces and behold, he has become wealthy. In learning to secure his one definite small desire he hath trained himself to secure a larger one. This is the process by which wealth is accumulated; first in small sums, then in larger ones as a man learns and becomes more capable.

"Desires must be simple and definite. They defeat their own purpose should they be too many, too confusing, or beyond the training to accomplish.

"As a man perfecteth himself in his calling even so doth his ability to earn increase. In those days when I was a humble scribe carving upon the clay for a few coppers each day, I observed that other workers did more than I and were paid more. Therefore, did I determine that I would be exceeded by none. Nor did it take long for me to discover the reason for their greater success. More interest in my work, more concentration upon my task, more persistence in my effort, and behold, few men could carve more tablets in a day than I. With reasonable promptness my increased skill was rewarded, nor was it necessary for me to go six times to my master to request recognition.

"The more of wisdom we know, the more we may earn. That man who seeks to learn more of his craft shall be richly rewarded. If he is an artisan, he may seek to learn the methods and the tools of those most skillful in the same line. If he laboreth at the law or at healing, he may consult and exchange knowledge with others of his calling. If he be a merchant, he may continually seek better goods that can be purchased at lower prices.

"Always do the affairs of man change and improve because keen minded men seek greater skill that they may better serve those upon whose patronage they depend. Therefore, I urge all men to be in the front rank of progress and not to stand still, lest they be left behind.

"Many things come to make a man's life rich with gainful experiences. Such things as the following, a man must do if he shall respect himself:

"He must pay his debts with all promptness within his power, not purchasing that for which he is unable to pay.

"He must take care of his family that they may think and speak well of him.

"He must make a will of record that in case the Gods call him, proper and honorable division of his property be accomplished.

"He must have compassion upon those who are injured or smitten by misfortune and aid them within reasonable limits. He must do deeds of thoughtfulness to those dear to him.

"Thus the seventh and last remedy for a lean purse is to cultivate thy own powers, to study and become wiser, to become more skillful, to so act as to respect thyself. **Thereby shalt thou acquire confidence in thyself to achieve thy carefully considered desires.**

"These then are the Seven Remedies for a Lean Purse, which, out of the experience of a long and successful life I do urge for all men who desire wealth.

"**There is MORE GOLD in BABYLON, my students, than thou dreamest of. There is abundance for all.**

"**Go thou forth and practice these truths that thou mayest prosper and grow wealthy, as is thy right.**

"**Go thou forth and teach these truths that every honorable subject of his majesty may also share liberally in the ample wealth of our beloved city. THIS IS THY KING'S COMMAND!**"

AFTER FAILURE— WHAT?

Orison Swett Marden

A great many people never really discover themselves until ruin stares them in the face. They do not seem to know how to bring out their reserves until they are overtaken by an overwhelming disaster, or until the sight of their blighted prospects and of the wreck of their homes and happiness stirs them to the very center of their beings.

The real test of character is what a man does after he fails. What will he do next? What resources, what inventiveness, will his failure arouse in him? Will it discover new sources of power, will it bring out reserves, double his determination, or will it dishearten him?

"I know no such unquestionable badge and ensign of a sovereign mind," said Emerson, "as that tenacity of purpose which, through all changes of companions, or parties, or fortunes, changes never, bates no jot of heart or hope, but wearies out opposition and arrives at its port."

"To come up again and wrest triumph from defeat." That is the secret of the success of every brave and noble life that ever was lived.

A little boy was asked how he learned to skate. "Oh, by getting up every time I fell down," he replied. This is the spirit that leads men and armies to victory. It is not the fall, but the not getting up, that is defeat.

Perhaps the past has been a bitter disappointment to you. In looking it over you may feel that you have been plodding along in mediocrity. You may not have succeeded in the particular things you expected to succeed in; or you may have lost friends and relatives who were very dear to you. You may have lost your business, and even your home may have been wrenched from you because you could not pay the mortgage on it, or because of sickness and consequent inability to work. The new year may present a very discouraging outlook to you. Yet, in spite of any or all of these misfortunes, if you refuse to be conquered, victory is awaiting you farther on the road.

This is the test of your manhood: how much is there left in you after you have lost everything outside of yourself? If you lie down now, throw up your hands, and acknowledge yourself worsted, there is not much in you. But if, with heart undaunted and face turned forward, you refuse to give up or to lose faith in yourself, if you scorn to beat a retreat, you will show that the man left in you is bigger than your loss, greater than your cross, and larger than any defeat.

You may say that you have failed too often, that there is no use in trying, that it is impossible for you to succeed, and that it is useless for you even to attempt to get on your feet again. Nonsense! There is no failure for a man whose spirit is unconquered. No matter how late the hour, or how many and repeated his failures, success is still possible. The evolution of Scrooge, the miser, in the closing years of his life, from a hard, narrow, heartless money-grubber, whose soul was imprisoned in his shining heap of hoarded gold, to a generous, genial lover of his kind, is no mere myth of Dickens' brain. Time and again, in the history of our daily lives, chronicled in our newspapers, recorded in biographies, or exhibited before our eyes, we see men and women redeeming past failures, rising up out of the stupor of discouragement, and boldly turning face forward once more.

There are thousands of people who have lost everything they had in the world who are just as far from failure as they were before their loss, because of their unconquerable spirit—stout hearts that never quail.

In true manhood there is something which rises higher than worldly success or failure. No matter what reverses come to him, what disappointments or failures, a really great man rises superior to them. He never loses his equanimity. In the midst of storms and trials to which a weak nature would succumb, his serene soul, his calm confidence still assert themselves, so completely dominating all outward conditions that they have no power to harm him.

"What is defeat?" says Wendell Phillips. "Nothing but the first steps to something higher." Many a one has finally succeeded only because he has failed after repeated efforts. If he had never met defeat he would never have known any great victory. There is something in defeat which puts new determination into a man of mettle.

No, there is no failure for the man who realizes his power, who never knows when he is beaten; there is no failure for the determined endeavor, the unconquerable will. There is no failure for the man who gets up every time he falls, who rebounds like a rubber ball, who persists when every one else gives up, who pushes on when every one else turns back.

LIGHT ON LIFE'S DIFFICULTIES

James Allen

I, Truth, am thy Redeemer, come to Me;
    Lay down thy sin and pain and wild unrest;
And I will calm thy spirit's stormy sea,
    Pouring the oil of peace upon thy breast:
Friendless and lone—lo, I abide with thee.

Defeated and deserted, cast away,
    What refuge hast thou? Whither canst thou fly?
Upon my changeless breast thy burdens lay;
    I am thy certain refuge, even I:
All things are passing; I alone can stay.

Lo I, the Great Forsaken, am the Friend
    Of the forsaken; I, whom men despise,
The weak, the helpless, and despised defend;
    I gladden aching hearts and weeping eyes;
Rest thou in Me, I am thy sorrow's end.

Lovers and friends and wealth, pleasures and fame—
    These fail and change, and pass into decay;
But My Love does not change; and in thy blame
    I blame thee not, nor turn my face away:
In My calm bosom hide thy sin and shame.

FOREWORD

When a man enters a dark room he is not sure of his movements; he cannot see the objects around, or properly locate them, and is liable to hurt himself by coming into sudden contact with them; but let a light be introduced, and immediately all confusion disappears, every object is seen, and there is no more danger of being hurt.

To the majority life is such a dark room, and their frequent hurts—their disappointments, perplexities, sorrows, and pains—are caused by sudden contact with principles which they do not see, and are therefore not prepared to deal with; but when the light of wisdom is introduced into the darkened understanding, confusion vanishes, difficulties are dissolved, all things are seen in their true place and proportion, and henceforth the man walks, open-eyed and unhurt, in the clear light of a wise comprehension.

JAMES ALLEN
Bryngoleu,
Ilfracombe, England

CONTENTS

THE LIGHT THAT LEADS
TO PERFECT PEACE

This book is intended to be a strong and kindly companion, as well as a source of spiritual renewal and inspiration to those who aim at a life well-lived and made strong and serene. It will help its readers to transform themselves into the ideal character thy would wish to be, and to make their life here that blessed thing which the majority only hope for in some future life.

Our life is what we make it by our own thoughts and deeds. It is our own state and attitude of mind which determine whether we are happy or unhappy, strong or weak, sinful or holy, foolish or wise. If one is unhappy, that state of mind belongs to himself, and is originated within himself; it is a state which responds to certain outward happenings, but its *cause* lies within, and not in those outward occurrences. If one is weak in will, he has brought himself to, and remains in, that condition by the course of thought and action which he has chosen and is still choosing. If one is sinful, it is because he has committed, and continues to commit, sinful acts. If he is foolish, it is because he himself does foolish things.

A man has no character, no soul, no life apart from his thoughts and deeds. What they are, that he is. As they are modified, so does he change. He is endowed with will, and can modify his character. As the carpenter changes the block of wood into a beautiful piece of furniture, so can the erring and sin-stricken man change himself into a wise and truth-loving being.

Each man is responsible for the thoughts which he thinks and the acts which he does, for his state of mind, and the life which he lives. No power, no event, no circumstance can compel a man to evil and unhappiness. He himself is his own compeller. He thinks and acts by his own volition. No being, however wise and great—not even the Supreme—can make him good and happy. He himself must choose the good, and thereby find the happy.

And because of this—*that when a man wishes and wills* he can find the Good and the True, and enjoy its bliss and peace—there is eternal gladness in the Courts of Truth, and holy joy amongst the Perfect Ones.

The Gates of Heaven are forever open, and no one is prevented from entering by any will or power but his own; but no one can enter the Kingdom of Heaven so long as he is enamored of, and chooses, the seductions of hell, so long as he resigns himself to sin and sorrow.

There is a larger, higher, nobler, diviner life than that of sinning and suffering, which is so common—in which, indeed, nearly all are immersed—a life of victory over sin, and triumph over evil; a life wise and happy, benign and tranquil, virtuous and peaceful. This life can be found and lived now, and he who lives it is steadfast in the midst of change; restful among the restless; peaceful, though surrounded by strife. Should death confront him, he is calm; though assailed by persecution, he knows no bitterness, and his heart is compassionate and filled with rejoicing. In this supremely beautiful life there is no evil, sin and sorrow are ended, and aching hearts and weeping eyes are no more.

This life of triumph is not for those who are satisfied with any lower conditions; it is for those who thirst of it and are willing to achieve it; who are as eager for righteousness as the miser is for gold. It is always at hand, and is offered to all, and blessed are they who accept and embrace it; they will enter the World of Truth; they will find the Perfect Peace.

LIGHT ON FACTS AND HYPOTHESES

When freedom of thought and freedom of expression abound, there is much controversy and much confusion, yet it is from such controversial confusion that the simple facts of life emerge, attracting us with their eternal uniformity and harmony, and appealing forcibly to us with their invisible simplicity and truth.

We are living in such an age of freedom and mental conflict. Never were religious sects so numerous. Schools—philosophical, occult, and otherwise—abound, and each is eager for the perpetuation and dominance of its own explanation of the universe. The world is in a condition of mental ferment. Contradiction has reached the point of confusion, so that the earnest seeker for Truth can find no solid rock of refuge in the opposing systems which are presented to him, and is thereby thrown back upon himself, upon those incontrovertible facts of his own being which are ever with him,—which are, indeed, himself, his life.

Controversy is ranged around hypotheses, not around facts. Fact is fixed and final; hypothesis is variable and vanishing. In his present stage of development, man is not alive to the beautiful simplicity of facts, nor to the power of satisfaction which is inherent in them; he does not perceive the intrinsic loveliness of truth, but must add something to it; hence, when a fact is named, the question almost invariably arises, "How can you explain the fact?" and then follows a hypothesis which leads to another hypothesis, and so on and on until the fact is altogether lost sight of amid a mass of contradictory suppositions. Thus arise the sects and controversial schools.

The clear perception of one fact will lead to the perception of other facts, but a supposition, while appearing to elucidate a fact, does in reality cover it up. We cannot realize the stately splendor of Truth while playing with the gaudy and attractive toys of pretty hypotheses. Truth is not an opinion, nor can any opinion enlarge or adorn it. Fact and supposition are eternally separate, and the cleverest intellectual jugglery—while it may entertain and deceive even the elect—cannot in the slightest degree alter a fact or affect the nature of things-as-they-are. Because of this, the true teacher abandons the devious path of hypothesis, and deals only with the simple facts of life, fixing the attention of men upon these, instead of increasing confusion and intensifying wordy warfare by foisting another assumption upon a world already lost and bewildered in a maze of hypotheses.

The facts of life are ever before us, and can be understood and known if we but abandon our egotism and the blinding delusions which that egotism creates. Man need not go beyond his own being to find wisdom, and the facts of that being afford a sufficient basis on which to erect a temple of knowledge of such beauty and dimensions that it shall at once emancipate and glorify.

Man is; and as he thinks, so he is. A perception and realization of these two facts alone—of man's being and thinking—lead into a vast avenue of knowledge which cannot stop short of the highest wisdom and perfection. One of the reasons why men do not become wise is that they occupy themselves with interminable speculations about a *soul* separate from themselves—that is, from their own mind—and so blind themselves to their actual nature and being. The supposition of a separate soul veils the eyes of man so that he does not see himself, does not know his mentality, is unaware of the nature of his thoughts without which he would have no conscious life.

Man's life is actual; his thoughts are actual; his life is actual. To occupy ourselves with the investigation of things that are, is the way of wisdom. Man considered as above, beyond, and separate from mind and thought, is speculative and not actual, and to occupy ourselves with the study of things that are not, is the way of folly.

Man cannot be separated from his mind; his life cannot be separated from his thoughts. Mind, thought, and life are as inseparable as light, radiance, and color, and are no more in need of another factor to elucidate them than are light, radiance, and color. The facts are all-sufficient, and contain within themselves the groundwork of all knowledge concerning them.

Man as mind is subject to change. He is not something "made" and finally complete, but has within him the capacity for progress. By the universal law of evolution he has *become* what he is, and is becoming that which he will be. His being is modified by every thought he thinks. Every experience affects his character. Every effort he makes changes his mentality. Herein is the secret of man's degradation, and also of his power and salvation if he but utilize this law of change in the right choice of thought.

To live is to think and act, and to think and act is to change. While man is ignorant of the nature of thought, he continues to change for better or worse; but, being acquainted with the nature of thought, he intelligently accelerates and directs the process of change, and only for the better.

What the sum total of a man's thoughts are, that he is. From the sameness of thought with man there is not the slightest fractional deviation. There is a change of result with the addition and subtraction of thought, but the mathematical law is an invariable quantity.

Seeing that man is mind, that mind is composed of thought, and that thought is subject to change, it follows the deliberately to change the thought is to change the man.

All religions work upon the heart, the thought of man, with the object of directing it into purer and higher channels; and success in this direction, whether partial or complete, is called "salvation"—that is, deliverance from one kind of thought, one condition of mind, by the substitution of another thought, another condition. It is true that the dispensers of religion to-day do not know this because of the hypothetical veil which intervenes between the fact and their consciousness; but they *do* it without knowing it, and the Great Teachers who founded the various religions, built upon this fact, as their precepts plainly show. The chief things upon which these Teachers lay such stress, and so constantly reiterate—such as the purification of the heart, the thinking of right thoughts, and the doing of good deeds—what are they but calls to a higher, nobler mode of thought-energizing forces urging men to effort in the choosing of thoughts which shall lift them into realms of greater power, greater good, greater bliss?

Aspiration, meditation, devotion—these are the chief means which men in all ages employ to reach up to higher modes of thought, wide airs of peace, vaster realms of knowledge, for "as he thinketh in his heart, so is he"; he is saved from himself—from his own folly and suffering— by creating within new habits of thoughts, by becoming a new thinker, a new man.

Should a man by a supreme effort succeed in thinking

as Jesus thought—not by imitation, but by a sudden realization of his indwelling power—he would be as Jesus. In the Buddhistic records there is an instance of a man, not the possessor of great piety or wisdom, who asked Buddha how one might attain the highest wisdom and enlightenment, and Buddha replied, "by ceasing from all desire"; and it is recorded that the man let go all personal desires and at once realized the highest wisdom and enlightenment. One of the sayings of Buddha runs, "The only miracle with which a wise man concerns himself is the transformation of a sinner into a saint," and Emerson referred to this transforming power of change of thought when he said:—

"It is as easy to be great as to be small,"

which is closely akin to that other great and oft-repeated but little understood saying:—

"Be ye therefore perfect, even as your Father which is in Heaven is perfect."

And, after all, what is the fundamental difference between a great man and a small one? It is one of thought, of mental attitude. True, it is one of knowledge, but then, knowledge cannot be separated from thought; and every substitution of a better for a worse thought is a transforming agency which marks an important advance in knowledge. Throughout the whole range of human life, from the lowest savage to the highest type of man, thought determines character, condition, knowledge.

The mass of humanity moves slowly along the evolutionary path urged by the blind impulse of its dominant thoughts as they are stimulated and called forth by external things; but the true thinker, the sage, travels swiftly and intelligently along a chosen path of his own. The multitudes, unenlightened concerning their spiritual nature, are the slaves of thought, but the sage is the master of thought. They follow blindly; he chooses intelligently. They obey the impulse of the moment, thinking of their immediate pleasure and happiness; he commands and subdues impulse, resting upon that which is permanently right. They, obeying blind impulse, violate the law of righteousness; he, conquering impulse, obeys the law of righteous. The sage stands face to face with the facts of life. He knows the nature of thought. He understands and obeys the law of his being.

But the sorrow-burdened victim of blind impulse can open his mental eyes and see the true nature of things when he wishes to do so. The sage—intelligent, radiant, calm—and the fool—confused, darkened, disturbed—are one in essence, and are divided only by the nature of their thoughts; when the fool turns away from and abandons his foolish thoughts and chooses and adopts wise thoughts, lo! he becomes a sage.

Socrates saw the essential oneness of virtue and knowledge, and so every sage sees. Learning may aid and accompany wisdom, but it does not lead to it. Only the choosing of wise thoughts, and necessarily, the doing of wise deeds, leads to wisdom. A man may be learned in the schools, but foolish in the school of life. Not the committing of words to memory, but the establishing oneself in purer thoughts, nobler thinking, leads to the peace-giving revelations of true knowledge.

Folly and wisdom, ignorance and enlightenment, are not merely the result of thought, they are thought itself. Both cause and effect—effort and result—are contained in thought.

> "All that we are is the result of what we have thought.
> It is founded on our thoughts; it is made up of our
>   thoughts."

Man is not a being possessing a soul, another self. He himself is soul. He himself is the thinker and doer, actor and knower. His composite mentality is himself. His spiritual nature is rounded by his sphere of thought. He it is that desires and sorrows, enjoys and suffers, loves and hates. The mind is not the instrument of a metaphysical, superhuman soul. Mind is soul; mind is being; mind is men.

Man can find himself. He can see himself as he is. When he is prepared to turn from the illusory and self-created world of hypothesis in which he wanders, and to stand face to face with actuality, then will be known himself as he is; moreover, he can picture himself as he would wish to be and can create within him the new thinker, the new man; for every moment is the time of choice—and every hour is destiny.

LIGHT ON THE LAW OF CAUSE AND EFFECT IN HUMAN LIFE

How frequently people associate the word "law" with hardness and cruelty! It seems to embody, for them, nothing but an inflexible tyranny. This arises partly from their inability to perceive principles apart from persons, and partly from the idea that the office of law is solely to punish. Viewed from such an attitude of mind, the term *law* is hazily regarded as some sort of indefinite personality whose business it is to hunt transgressors and crush them with overwhelming punishments.

Now while law punishes, its primary office is to *protect*. Even the laws which man makes, are framed by him to protect himself from his own baser passions. The law of our country is instituted for the protection of life and property, and it only comes into operation as a punishing factor when it is violated. Offenders against it probably think of it as cruel, and doubtless regard it with terror, but to them that obey it, it is an abiding protector and friend, and can hold for them no terror.

So with the Divine Law which is the stay of the Universe, the heart and life of the Cosmos—it is that which protects and upholds, and it is no less protective in its penalties than in its peaceful blessings; it is, indeed, an eternal protection which is never for one moment withheld, and it shields all beings against themselves by bringing all violations of itself, whether ignorant or willful, through pain to nothingness.

Law cannot be partial. It is an unvarying mode of action, disobeying which, we are hurt; obeying, we are made happy. Neither protestation nor supplication can alter it, for if it could be altered or annulled the universe would collapse and chaos would prevail.

It is not less kind that we should suffer the penalty of our wrongdoing than that we should enjoy the blessedness of our right-doing. If we could escape the effects of our ignorance and sin, all security would be gone, and there would be no refuge, for we could then be equally doubtful of the result of our wisdom and goodness. Such a scheme would be one of caprice and cruelty, whereas law is a method of justice and kindness.

Indeed, the supreme law is the principle of eternal kindness, faultless in working, and infinite in application. It is none other than that.

"Eternal Love, forever full,
Forever flowing free,"

of which the Christian sings; and the "Boundless Compassion" of Buddhistic precepts and poetry. The law which punishes us is the law which preserves us. When in their ignorance men would destroy themselves, its everlasting arms are thrown about them in loving, albeit sometimes painful, protection. Every pain we suffer brings us nearer to the knowledge of the Divine Wisdom. Every blessing we enjoy speaks to us of the perfection of the Great Law, and of the fulness of bliss that shall be man's when he has come to his heritage of Divine Knowledge. We progress by learning, and we learn, up to a certain point, by suffering. When the heart is mellowed by love, the law of love is perceived in all its wonderful kindness; when wisdom is acquired, peace is assured.

We cannot alter the law of things, which is of sublime perfection, but we can alter ourselves so as to comprehend more and more of that perfection, and make its grandeur ours. To wish to bring down the perfect to the imperfect is the height of folly, but to strive to bring the imperfect up to the perfect is the height of wisdom.

Seers of the Cosmos do not mourn over the scheme of things. They see the universe as a perfect whole, and not as an imperfect jumble of parts. The Great Teachers are men of abiding joy and heavenly peace.

The blind captive of unholy desire may cry:

"Ah! Love; could you and I with him conspire
To grasp this sorry scheme of things entire,

Would we not shatter it to bits, and then
Remould it nearer to the heart's desire?"

This is the wish of the voluptuary, the wish to enjoy unlawful pleasures to any extent, and not reap any painful consequences. It is such men who regard the universe as a "sorry scheme of things." They want the universe to bend to their will and desire; want lawlessness, not law; but the wise man bends his will and subjects his desires to the Divine Order, and he sees the universe as the glorious perfection of an infinitude of parts.

Buddha always referred to the moral law of the universe as the Good Law, and indeed it is not rightly perceived if it is thought of as anything but good; for in it there can be no grain of evil, no element of unkindness. It is no iron-hearted monster crushing the weak and destroying the ignorant, but a soothing love and brooding compassion shielding the tenderest from harm, and protecting the strongest from a too destructive use of their strength. It destroys all evil, it preserves all good. It enfolds the tiniest seedling in its care, and it destroys the most colossal wrong with a breath. To perceive it, is the beatific vision; to know it, is the beatific bliss; and they who perceive and know it are at peace; they are glad forever more.

"Such is the law which moves to righteousness,
Which none at last can turn aside or stay;
The heart of it is love; the end of it
Is peace and consummation sweet: obey."

LIGHT ON VALUES—
SPIRITUAL AND MATERIAL

It is an old-time axiom that "everything has its price." Everybody knows this commercially, but how few know it spiritually. Business consists of a mutual interchange of equitable values. The customer gives money and receives goods, and the merchant gives goods and receives money. This method is universal, and is regarded by all as just. In spiritual things the method is the same, but the form of interchange is different. For material things a material thing is given in exchange, but for spiritual things a spiritual thing is given in exchange. Now these two forms of exchange cannot be transposed; they are of reverse natures, and remain eternally separate. Thus a man may take a sovereign to a shop and ask for a pound's worth of food, or clothing, or literature, and he will receive goods to the value of his sovereign; but if he were to take a sovereign to a teacher of Truth, and ask to be supplied with a pound's worth of religion, or righteousness, or wisdom, he would be told that those things cannot be purchased with money, that their spiritual nature excludes them from material business transactions. The wise teacher, however, would also tell him that these spiritual necessities *must* be purchased, that though money cannot buy them, yet they have their price, that something must be parted with before they can be received, that, in a word, instead of offering money he must offer up self, or selfishness. For so much selfishness given up, so much religion, righteousness, and wisdom would be immediately received, and this without fail, and with perfect equity, for if a man is sure of receiving perishable material food and clothing for the money he puts down, how much more surely will he receive the imperishable spiritual sustenance and protection for the selfishness which he lays down! Shall the law operate in the lesser, and fail in the greater? Man may fail to observe the law, but the law is infallible.

A man may love his money, but he must part with it before he can receive the material comforts of life. Likewise a man may love his selfish gratifications, but he must give them up before he can receive the spiritual comforts of religion.

Now when a tradesman gives goods for money, it is not that he may keep the money, but that he may give it in exchange for other goods. The primary function of business is not to enable everybody to hoard up money, but to facilitate the interchange of commodities. The miser is the greatest of all failures, and he may die of starvation and exposure while being a millionaire, because he is a worshipper of the letter of money, and an ignorer of its spirit—the spirit of mutual interchange. Money is a means, not an end; its exchange is a sign that goods are being justly given and received. Thus commerce, with all its innumerable ramifications of detail, is reducible to one primary principle, namely:

Mutual interchange of the material necessities of life.

Now let us follow this principle into the spiritual sphere, and trace there its operation. When a religious man gives spiritual things—kindness, sympathy, love—and receives happiness in return, it is not that he may hoard and hug to himself that happiness, but that he may give it to others, and so receive back spiritual things. The primary function of religion is not to enable all to hoard up personal pleasure, but to render actual the interchange of spiritual blessings. The most selfish man—he whose chief object is the getting of happiness for himself—is a spiritual miser, and his mind may perish of spiritual destitution though he be surrounded with the objects which he has obtained to pander to his pleasure, because he is worshipping the letter of happiness, and is ignoring its spirit— the spirit of unselfish interchange. The object of selfishness is the getting of personal pleasure, or happiness; the object of religion is the diffusion of virtue. Thus religion, with all its innumerable creeds, may be resolved into one primary principle, namely:

Mutual interchange of spiritual blessings.

What, then, are the spiritual blessings? They are kindness, brotherliness, goodwill, sympathy, forbearance, patience, trustfulness, peacefulness, love unending, and compassion unlimited. These blessings, these necessities for the starving spirit of man, can be obtained, but their price *must* be paid; unkindness, uncharitableness, ill-will, hardness, ill-temper, impatience, suspicion, strife, hatred, and cruelty—all these, along with the happiness, the personal satisfaction, which they give must be yielded up. These spiritual coins, dead in themselves, must be parted with, and when parted with, there will be immediately received their spiritual counterparts, the living and imperishable blessings to which they are a means and of which they are a sign.

To conclude, when a man gives money to a merchant, and receives goods in return, he does not wish to have his money again. He has willingly parted with it forever, and is satisfied with the exchange. So when a man gives up unrighteousness in exchange for righteousness, he does not wish to have his selfish pleasures back again. He has given them up forever, and is satisfied and in peace.

Thus also, when one bestows a gift, even though it be a material gift, he does not look for the receiver to send him back its value in money, because it is a religious deed, and not a business transaction. The material thing thus given represents the interchange of a spiritual blessing, and its accompanying bliss, the bliss of a gift bestowed, and that of a gift received.

"Are not two sparrows sold for a farthing?" Everything in the universe—every object and every thought—is valued. Material things have a material value, spiritual things have a spiritual value, and to confound these values is not wise. To seek to purchase spiritual blessings with money, or material luxuries with virtue, is the way of selfishness and folly. It is to confound barter with religion, and to make a religion of barter. Sympathy, kindness, love cannot be bought and sold, they can only be given and received. When a gift is paid for, it ceases to be a gift.

Because everything has a value, that which is freely given is gained with accumulation. He who gives up the lesser happiness of selfishness, gains the greater happiness of unselfishness. The universe is just, and its justice is so perfect that he who has once perceived it can no more doubt or be afraid, he can only wonder and be glad.

LIGHT ON THE SENSE
OF PROPORTION

In a nightmare there is no relation of one thing to another; all things are haphazard, and there is general confusion and misery. Wise men have likened the self-seeking life to a nightmare; and there is a close resemblance between a selfish life, in which the sense of proportion is so far lost that things are only seen as they affect one's own selfish aims, and in which there are feverish excitements and overwhelming troubles and disasters, and that state of troubled sleep known as nightmare.

In a nightmare, too, the controlling will and perceiving intelligence are asleep; and in a selfish life the better nature and spiritual perceptions are locked in profound slumber.

The uncultivated mind lacks the sense of proportion. It does not see the right relation of one natural object to another, and is therefore dead to the beauty and harmony with which it is surrounded.

And what is this sense of proportion but the faculty of *seeing things as they are!* It is a faculty which needs cultivating, and its cultivation, when applied to natural objects, embraces the entire intelligence and refines the moral nature. It enters, however, into spiritual things as well as things natural, and here is more lacking, and more greatly needed; for to see things as they are in the spiritual sphere, is to find no ground for grief, no lodging place for lamentation.

Whence spring all this grief and anxiety, and fear and trouble? Is it not because things are not as men wish them to be? Is it not because the multiplicity of desires prevents them from seeing things in their true perspective and right proportion?

When one is overwhelmed with grief, he sees nothing but his loss, its nearness to him blots out the whole view of life. The thing in itself may be small, but to the sufferer it assumes a magnitude which is out of all proportion to the surrounding objects of life.

All who have passed the age of thirty, can look back over their lives at times when they were perplexed with anxiety, overwhelmed with grief, or even, perhaps, on the verge of despair, over incidents which, seen now in their right proportion, are known to be very small.

If the would-be suicide will to-day stay his hand, and wait, he will at the end of ten years marvel at his folly over so comparatively small a matter.

When the mind is possessed by passion or paralyzed with grief, it has lost the power of judgment, it cannot weigh and consider, it does not perceive the relative values and proportions of the things by which it is disturbed; awake and acting, it yet moves in a nightmare which holds its faculties in thrall.

The passionate partisan lacks this sense of proportion to such an extent, that to him his own side or view appears all that is right and good, and his opponent's all that is bad and wrong. To this partiality his reason is chained, so that whatever reason he may bring to bear upon the matter, is enlisted in the service of bias, and is not exercised in order to find the just relation which exists between the two sides. He is so convinced that his own party is all right, and the other, equally intelligent, party is all wrong, that it is impossible for him to be impartial and just. The only thing he understands as justice is that of getting his own way, or placing some ruling power in the hands of his party.

Just as the sense of proportion in things material puts an end to the spirit of repugnance, so in things spiritual it puts an end to the spirit of strife. The true artist does not see ugliness anywhere, he sees only beauty. That which is loathsome to others, fills, to him, its rightful place in nature, and it appears in his picture as a thing of beauty. The true seer does not see evil anywhere, he sees universal good. That which is hateful to others, he sees in its rightful place in the scheme of evolution, and it is held dispassionately in his mind as an object of contemplation.

Men worry, and grieve, and fight, because they lack this sense of proportion, because they do not see things in their right relations. The objects of their turbulence are not things-in-themselves, but their own opinions about things, self-created shadows, the unreal creations of an egoistic nightmare.

The cultivation and development of the ethical sense of proportion converts the heated partisan into the gentle peacemaker, and gives the calm and searching eye of the prophet to the hitherto blind instrument in the clashing play of selfish forces.

The spiritual sense of proportion gives sanity; it restores the mind to calmness; it bestows impartiality and justice, and reveals a universe of faultless harmony.

LIGHT ON ADHERENCE
TO PRINCIPLE

The man of Truth never departs from the divine principles which he has espoused. He may be threatened with sickness, poverty, pain, loss of friends and position, yea, even with immediate death, yet he does not desert the principles which he knows to be eternally true. To him, there is one thing more grievous, more to be feared and shunned than all the above evils put together, and that is—*the desertion of principle*. To turn coward in the hour of trial, to deny conscience, to join the rabble of passions, desires, and fears, in turning upon, accusing, and crucifying the Eternal Christ of Divine Principle, because, forsooth, that principle has not given him personal health, affluence and ease—this, to the man of Truth, is the evil of evils, the sin of sins.

We cannot escape sickness and death. Though we avoid them for a long time, in the end they will overtake us. But we can escape wrong-doing, we can avoid fear and cowardice; and when we eschew wrong doing and cast out fear, the evils of life will not subdue us when they overtake us, for we shall have mastered them; instead of avoiding them for a season we shall have conquered them on their own ground.

There are those who teach that it is right to do wrong when that wrong is to protect another; that it is good, for instance, to tell a lie when its object is the well-being of another—that is, that it is right to desert the principle of truthfulness under severe trial. Such teaching has never emanated from the lips of the Great Teachers. It has not been uttered even by those lesser, yet superbly noble men, the prophets, saints, and martyrs, for these divinely illuminated men knew full well that no circumstance can make a wrong a right, and that a lie has no saving and protective power. Wrong-doing is a greater evil than pain, and a lie is more deadly and destructive than death. Jesus rebuked Peter for trying to shield his Master's life by wrong-doing, and no right-minded person would accept life at the expense of the moral character of another when it appeared possible to do so.

All men admire and revere the martyrs, those steadfast men and women who feared wrong, cowardice, and lying, but who did not fear pain and death; who were steadfast and calm in their adherence to principle even when brought to the utmost extremity of trial, yea, even when the taunts and jeers of enemies assailed them, and the tears and agonies of loved ones appealed to them, they flinched not nor turned back, knowing that the future good and salvation of the whole world depended upon their firmness in that supreme hour; and for this, they stand through all time as monuments of virtue, centres of saving and uplifting power for all humankind. But he who lied to save himself, or for the sake of the two or three beings whom he personally loved, is rarely heard of, for in that hour of desertion of principle, his power was gone; and if he *is* heard of, he is not loved for that lie; he is always looked upon as one who fell when the test was applied; as an example of the highest virtue he is rejected by all men in all times.

Had all men believed that an untruth was right under extreme circumstances, we should have had no martyrs and saints, the moral fibre of humanity would have been undermined, and the world left to grope in ever deepening darkness.

The attitude which regards wrong-doing for the sake of others as the right thing to do, is based on the tacit assumption that wrong and untruth are inferior evils to unhappiness, pain, and death; but the man of moral insight knows that wrong and untruth are the greater evils, and so he never commits them, even though his own life or the lives of others appear to be at stake.

It is easy for a man in the flowery time of ease or the heyday of prosperity to persuade himself that he is staunchly adhering to principle, but when pain overtakes him, when the darkness of misfortune begins to settle down upon him, and the pressure of circumstances hems him in—then he is on his trial, then he has come to his testing time; in that season it will be brought to the light whether he clings to self or adheres to Truth.

Principles are for our salvation in the hour of need. If we desert them in that hour, how can we be saved from the snares and pains of self?

If a man does wrong to his conscience, thinking thereby to avoid some immediate pain or pressing evil, he does but increase pain and evil. The good man is less anxious to avoid pain than wrong-doing.

There is neither wisdom nor safety in deserting permanent and protective principles when our happiness seems to be at stake. If we desert the true for the pleasant, we shall lose both the pleasant and the true; but if we desert the pleasant for the true, the peace of truth will soothe away our sorrow. If we barter the higher for the lower, emptiness and anguish will overtake us, and then, having abandoned the Eternal, where is our rock of refuge? But if we yield up the lower for the higher, the strength and satisfaction of the higher will remain with us, fulness of joy will overtake us, and we shall find in truth a rock of refuge from the evils and sorrows of life.

To find the permanent amid all the changes of life, and, having found it, adhere to it under all circumstances—this only is true happiness, this only is salvation and lasting peace.

LIGHT ON THE SACRIFICE
OF THE SELF

Self-sacrifice is one of the fundamental principles in the teaching of all the Great Spiritual Masters. It consists in yielding up self, or selfishness, so that Truth may become the source of conduct. Self is not an entity that has to be cast out, but a condition of mind that has to be converted. The renunciation of self is not the annihilation of intelligent being, but the annihilation of every dark and selfish desire. Self is the blind clinging to perishable things and transient pleasures as distinguished from the intelligent practice of virtue and righteousness. Self is the lusting, coveting, desiring of the heart, and it is this that must be yielded up before Truth can be known, with its abiding calm and endless peace.

To give up *things* will not avail; *it is the lust for things* that must be sacrificed. Though a man sacrifice wealth, position, friends, fame, home, wife, child—yea, and life also—

it will not avail if self is not renounced. Buddha renounced the world and all that it held dear to him, but for six years he wandered and searched and suffered, and not till he yielded up the desires of his heart did he become enlightened and arrive at peace.

By giving up only the *objects* of self-indulgence, no peace will ensue, but torment will follow. It is self-indulgence, *the desire for the object*, that must be abandoned—then peace enters the heart.

Sacrifice is painful so long as there is any vestige of self remaining in the heart. While there remains in the heart a lurking desire for an unworthy object or pleasure that has been sacrificed, there will be periods of intense suffering, and fierce temptation; but when the *desire* for the unworthy object or pleasure is put away forever from the mind, and the sacrifice is complete and perfect, then, concerning that particular object or pleasure, there can be no more suffering or temptation. So when self in its entirety is sacrificed, sacrifice, in its painful aspect, is at an end, and perfect knowledge and perfect peace are reached.

Hatred is self; covetousness is self; envy and jealousy are self; malice is self; pride and superciliousness are self; vanity and boasting are self; gluttony and sensuality are self; lying and deception are self; speaking evil of one's neighbor is self; anger and revenge are self. Self-sacrifice consists in yielding up all these dark conditions of mind and heart. The process is a painful one in its early stages, but soon a divine peace descends at intervals upon the pilgrim; later, this peace remains longer with him, and finally, when the rays of Truth begin to be shed abroad in the heart, remains with him.

This sacrifice leads to peace; for in the perfect life of Truth, there is no more sacrifice, and no more pain and sorrow; for where there is no more self there is nothing to be given up; where there is no clinging of the mind to perishable things there is nothing to be renounced; where all has been laid upon the altar of Truth, selfish love is swallowed up in divine love; and in divine love there is no thought of self, for there is the perfection of insight, enlightenment, and immortality, and therefore perfect peace.

LIGHT ON THE
MANAGEMENT OF
THE MIND

Following the last chapter a few hints on the management of one's mind will doubtless be opportune. Before a man can see even the necessity for thorough and complete self-government, he will have to throw off a great delusion in which so many are involved—the delusion of believing that his lapses of conduct are due to those about him, and not entirely to himself. "I could make far greater progress if I were not hindered by others," or "It is impossible for me to make any headway, seeing that I live with such irritable people," are commonly expressed complaints which spring from the error of imagining that others are responsible for one's own folly.

The violent or irritable man always blames those about him for his fits of anger, and by continually living in this delusion, he becomes more and more confirmed in his

rashness and perturbations, for how can a man overcome—nay, how can he even try to overcome, his weakness if he convinces himself that it springs entirely from
the actions of others? Moreover, firmly believing this, as
he does, he vents his anger more and more upon others
in order to try and make matters better for himself, and
so becomes completely lost to all knowledge of the real
origin of his unhappy state.

> "Men cast the blame of their unprosperous acts
> Upon the abettors of their own resolve,
> Or anything but their weak guilty selves."

All a man's weaknesses and sins and falls take their rise
in his own heart, and he alone is responsible for them. It
is true there are tempters and provokers, but temptations
and provocations are powerless to him who refuses to respond to them. Tempters and provokers are but foolish
men, and he who gives way to them has become a willing co-operator in their folly; he is unwise and weak, and
the source of his troubles is in himself. The pure man cannot be tempted; the wise man cannot be provoked.

Let a man fully realize that he is absolutely responsible
for his every action, and he has already gone a considerable distance along the path which leads to wisdom and
peace, for he will then commence to utilize temptation as
a means of growth, and the wrong conduct of others he
will regard as a test of his own strength.

Socrates thanked the gods for the gift of a shrewish

wife in that it enabled him the better to cultivate the virtue of patience; and it is a simple and easily perceived truth that we can the better grow patient by living with the impatient, better grow unselfish by living with the selfish. If a man is impatient with the impatient, he is himself impatient; if he is selfish with the selfish, then he is himself selfish. The test and measure of virtue is trial, and, like gold and precious stones, the more it is tested the brighter it shines. If a man thinks he has a virtue, yet gives way when its opposing vice is presented to him, let him not delude himself, he has not yet attained to the possession of that virtue.

If a man would rise and become a man indeed, let him cease to think the weak and foolish thought, "I am hindered by others," and let him set about to discover that he is hindered only by himself; let him realize that the giving way to another is but a revelation of his own imperfection, and lo! upon him will descend the light of wisdom, and the door of peace will open unto him, and he will soon become the conqueror of self.

The fact that a man is continually troubled and disturbed by close contact with others, is an indication that he requires such contact to impel him onward to a clearer comprehension of himself, and toward a higher and more steadfast state of mind. The very things which he regards as insurmountable hindrances will become to him the most valuable aids when he fully realizes his moral responsibility and his innate power to do right. He will then cease to blame others for his unmanly conduct, and will commence to live steadfastly under all circumstances; the scales of self-delusion will quickly fall from his eyes, and he will then see that ofttimes when he imagined himself provoked by others, he himself was really the provoker; and as he rises above his own mental perturbations, the necessity for coming in contact with the same conditions in others will cease, and he will pass, by a natural process, into the company of the good and pure, and will then awaken in others the nobility which he has arrived at in himself.

"Be noble! and the nobleness that lies
In other men, sleeping, but never dead,
Will rise in majesty to meet thine own."

LIGHT ON SELF-CONTROL: THE DOOR OF HEAVEN

The foremost lesson which the world has to learn on its way to wisdom, is the lesson of self-control. All the bitter punishments which men undergo in the school of experience are inflicted because they have failed to learn this lesson. Apart from self-control, salvation is a meaningless word, and peace is an impossibility; for how can a man be saved from any sin whilst he continues to give way to it? or how can he realize abiding peace until he has conquered and subdued the troubles and perturbations of his mind?

Self-control is the Door of Heaven; it leads to light and peace. Without it a man is already in hell; he is lost in darkness and unrest. Men inflict upon themselves far-reaching sufferings, and pass through indescribable torments, both of body and soul, through lack of self-control; and not until they resort to its practice can their sufferings and torments pass away, for it has no substitute, nothing can take its place, and there is no power in the universe that can do for a man that which he, sooner or later, *must* do for himself, by entering upon the practice of self-control.

By self-control a man manifests his divine power and ascends toward divine wisdom and perfection. Every man can practise it. The weakest man can begin now, and until he does begin, his weakness will remain, or he will become weaker still. Calling or not calling upon God or Jesus, Brahma or Buddha, Spirits or Masters, will not avail men who refuse to govern themselves and to purify their hearts. Believing or disbelieving that Jesus is God, that Buddha is omniscient, or the Spirits or Masters guide human affairs, cannot help men who continue to cling to the elements of strife and ignorance and corruption within themselves.

What theological affirmation or denial can justify, or what outward power put right, the man who refuses to abandon a slanderous or abusive tongue, or give up an angry temper, or to sacrifice his impure imaginings? The flower reaches the upper light by first contending with the under darkness, and man can only reach the Light of Truth by striving against the darkness within himself.

The vast importance of self-control is not realized by men, its absolute necessity is not apprehended by them, and the spiritual freedom and glory to which it leads are hidden from their eyes. Because of this, men are enslaved and misery and suffering ensue. Let a man contemplate the violence, impurity, disease, and suffering which obtain upon earth, and consider how much of it is due to want of self-control, and he will gradually come to realize the great need there is for self-control.

I say again, that self-control is the Gate of Heaven, for without it neither happiness nor love nor peace can be realized and maintained. In the degree that it is lacked by a man, in just that measure will his mind and life be given over to confusion, and it is because such a large number of individuals have not yet learned to practise it that the enforced restraint of national laws is required for the maintenance of order and the prevention of a destructive confusion. Self-control is the beginning of virtue, and it leads to the acquisition of every noble attribute; it is the first essential quality in a well-ordered and truly religious life, and it leads to calmness, blessedness, and peace. Without it, although there may be theological belief or profession, there can be no true religion, for what is religion but enlightened conduct? and what is spirituality but the triumph over the unruly tendencies of the mind?

When men both depart from and refuse to practise self-control, then they fall into the great and dark delusion of separating religion from conduct; then they persuade themselves that religion consists, not in overcoming self and living blamelessly, but in holding a certain belief about Scripture, and in worshipping a certain Saviour in a particular way; hence arise the innumerable complications and confusions of letter-worship, and the violence and bitter strife into which men fall in defence of their own formulated religion. But true religion cannot be formulated; it is purity of mind, a loving heart, a soul at peace with the world. It needs not to be defended, for it is Being and Doing and Living. A man begins to practise religion when he begins to control himself.

LIGHT ON ACTS AND THEIR CONSEQUENCES

One of the commonest excuses for wrong-doing is that if right were done calamity would ensue. Thus the foolish concern themselves, not with the act, but with the consequence of the act, a fore-knowledge of which is assumed. The desire to secure pleasant results, and to escape unpleasant consequences, is at the root of that confusion of mind which renders men incapable of distinguishing between good and evil, and prevents them from practising the one and abandoning the other. Even when it is claimed that the wrong thing is done, not for one's self, but in order to secure the happiness of others, the delusion is the same, only it is more subtle and dangerous.

The wise concern themselves with the act, and not with its consequences. They consider, not what is pleasant or unpleasant, but *what is right*. Thus doing what is right only, and not straining after results, they are relieved of all burdens of doubt, desire, and fear. Nor can one who so acts ever become involved in an inextricable difficulty, or be troubled with painful perplexity. His course is so simple, straight, and plain that he can never be confused with misgivings and uncertainties. Those who so act are said by Krishna to act "without regard to the fruits of action," and he further declares that those who have thus renounced results are supremely good, supremely wise.

Those who work for pleasant results only, and who depart from the right path when their, or others', happiness appears to be at stake, cannot escape doubt, difficulty, perplexity, and pain. Ever forecasting probable consequences, they act in one way to-day, and in another way to-morrow; unstable, and blown about by the changing winds of circumstance, they become more and more bewildered, and the consequences about which they trouble do not accrue.

But they who work for righteousness only, who are careful to do the right act, putting away all selfish considerations, all thought of results, they are steadfast, unchanging, untroubled and in peace amid all vicissitudes, and the fruits of their acts are ever sweet and blessed.

Even the knowledge, which only the righteous possess, that wrong acts can never produce good results, and that right acts can never bring about bad results, is in itself fraught with sweet assurance and peace. For whether the fruits of acts are sought or unsought, they cannot be escaped.

They who sow to self, and, ignorant of the law of Truth, think they can make their own results, reap the bitter fruits of self.

They who sow to righteousness, knowing themselves to be the reapers, *and not the makers of consequences*, reap the sweet fruits of righteousness.

Right is supremely simple, and is without complexity. Error is interminably complex, and involves the mind in confusion.

To put away self and passion, and establish one's self in right-doing, this is the highest wisdom.

LIGHT ON THE WAY
OF WISDOM

The Path of Wisdom is the highest way, the way in which all doubt and uncertainty are dispelled and knowledge and surety are realized.

Amid the excitements and pleasures of the world and the surging whirlpools of human passions, Wisdom—so calm, so silent and so beautiful—is indeed difficult to find, difficult, not because of its incomprehensible complexity, but because of its unobtrusive simplicity, and because self is so blind and rash, and so jealous of its rights and pleasures.

Wisdom is "rejected of men" because it always comes right home to one's self in the form of wounding reproof, and the lower nature of man cannot bear to be reproved. Before Wisdom can be acquired, self must be wounded to the death, and because of this, because Wisdom is the enemy of self, self rises in rebellion, and will not be overcome and denied.

The foolish man is governed by his passions and personal cravings, and when about to do anything he does not ask "Is this right?" but only considers how much pleasure or personal advantage he will gain by it. He does not govern his passions and act from fixed principles, but is the slave of his inclinations and follows where they lead.

The wise man governs his passions and puts away all personal cravings. He never acts from impulse and passion, but dispassionately considers what is right to be done, and does it. He is always thoughtful and self-possessed, and guides his conduct by the loftiest moral principles. He is superior to both pleasure and pain.

Wisdom cannot be found in books or travel, in learning or philosophy, it is *acquired by practice only*. A man may read the precepts of the greatest sages continually, but if he does not purify and govern himself he will remain foolish. A man may be intimately conversant with the writings of the greatest philosophers, but so long as he continues to give way to his passions he will not attain to wisdom.

Wisdom is right action, right doing; folly is wrong action, wrong doing. All reading, all study, all learning is vain if a man will not see his errors and give them up. Wisdom says to the vain man, "Do not praise yourself," to the proud man, "Humble yourself," to the gossip, "Govern your tongue," to the angry man, "Subdue your anger," to the resentful man, "Forgive your enemy," to the self-indulgent man, "Be temperate," to the impure man, "Purge your heart of lust," and to all men, "Beware of small faults, do your own duty faithfully, and never inter-meddle with the duty of another."

These things are very simple; the doing of them is simple, but as it leads to the annihilation of self, the selfish tendencies in man object to them and rise up in revolt against them, loving their own life of turbulent excitement and feverish pleasure, and hating the calm and beautiful silence of Wisdom. Thus men remain in folly.

Nevertheless, the Way of Wisdom is always open, is always ready to receive the tread of the pilgrim who has grown weary of the thorny and intricate ways of folly. No man is prevented from becoming wise but by himself; no man can acquire Wisdom but by his own exertions; and he who is prepared to be honest with himself, to measure the depths of his ignorance, to come face to face with his errors, to recognize and acknowledge his faults, and at once to set about the task of his own regeneration, such a man will find the way of Wisdom, walking which with humble and obedient feet, he will in due time come to the sweet City of Deliverance.

LIGHT ON DISPOSITION

I cannot help it, it is my disposition." How often one hears this expression as an excuse for wrong-doing. What does it imply? This, that the person who utters it believes that he has no choice in the matter, that he cannot alter his character. He believes that he must go on doing the wrong thing to the end of his days because he was "born so," or because his father or grandfather was like it; or, if not these, then some one along the family line a hundred, or two or three hundred years ago must have been afflicted, and therefore he is and must remain so. Such a belief should be uprooted, destroyed, and cast away, for it is not only without reason, it is a complete barrier to all progress, to all growth in goodness, to all development of character and noble expansion of life. Character is not permanent; it is, indeed, one of the most changeable things in nature. If not changed by a conscious act of the will, it is being continually modified and re-formed by the pressure of circumstances. Disposition is not fixed, except in so far as one fixes it by continuing to do the same thing, and by persistence in the stubborn belief that he "cannot help it." Immediately one gets rid of that belief he will find that he *can* help it; further, he will find that intelligence and will are instruments which can mould disposition to any extent, and that, too, with considerable rapidity if one is in earnest.

What is disposition but a habit formed by repeating the same thing over and over again? Cease repeating (doing) the thing, and lo! the disposition is changed, the character is altered. To cease from an old habit of thought or action is, I know, difficult at first, but with each added effort the difficulty decreases, and finally disappears, and then the new and good habit is formed and the disposition is changed from bad to good, the character is ennobled, the mind is delivered from torment and is lifted into joy.

There is no need for any one to remain the slave of a disposition which causes him unhappiness, and which he himself regards as undesirable. He can abandon it. He can break away from the slavery. He can deliver himself and be free.

LIGHT ON INDIVIDUAL LIBERTY

Within the sphere of his own mind man has all power, but in the sphere of other minds and outside things, his power is extremely limited. He can command his own mind, but he cannot command the mind of others. He can choose what he shall think, but he cannot choose what others shall think. He cannot control the weather as he wills, but he can control his mind, and decide what his mental attitude toward the weather shall be.

A man can reform the dominion of his own mind, but he cannot reform the outer world because that outer world is composed of other minds having the same freedom of choice as himself. A pure being cannot cleanse the heart of one less pure, but by his life of purity and by elucidating his experience in the attainment of purity, he can, as a teacher, act as a guide to others, and so enable them more readily and rapidly to purify themselves. But even then those others have all power to decide whether they shall accept or reject such guidance, so complete is man's choice.

It is because of this dual truth—that man has no power in the outer realm of others' minds and yet has all power over his own mind, that he cannot avoid the consequences of his own thoughts and acts. Man is altogether powerless to alter or avert consequences, but he is altogether powerful in his choice of causative thought. Having chosen his thoughts, he must accept their full consequences; having acted, he cannot escape the full results of his act.

Law reigns universally, and there is perfect individual liberty. A man can do as he likes, but all other men can do as they like. A man has power to steal, but others have power to protect themselves against the thief. Having sent out his thought, having acted his purpose, a man's power over that thought and purpose is at an end; the consequences are certain and cannot be escaped, and they will be of the nature of the thought and act which produced them—painful or blessed.

Seeing that a man can think and do as he chooses, and that all others have the like liberty, a man has to learn, sooner or later, to reckon with other minds, and until he does this he will be ceaselessly involved in suffering. To think and act apart from the consideration of others is both an abuse of power and an infringement of liberty. Such thoughts and acts are annulled and brought to nought by the harmonizing Principle of Liberty itself, and such annulling and bringing to nought is felt by the individual as suffering. When the mind, rising above ignorance, recognizes the magnitude of its power within its own sphere and, ceasing to antagonize itself against others, it harmonizes itself to those other minds, acknowledging their freedom of choice, then is realized spiritual plenitude and the cessation of suffering.

Selfishness, egotism, and despotism are, from the spiritual standpoint, transferable terms; they are one and the same thing. Every selfish thought or act is a manifestation of egotism, is an effort of despotism, and it is met with suffering and defeat: it is annulled because the Law of Liberty cannot, in the smallest particular, be annulled. If selfishness could conquer, Liberty would be non-existent, but selfishness fails of all results but pain, because Liberty is supreme. An act of selfishness contains two elements of egotism: namely, (1) the denial of the liberty of others, and (2) the assertion of one's own liberty beyond its legitimate sphere. It thereby destroys itself. Despotism is death.

Man is not the creature of selfishness, he is the maker of it; it is an indication of his power—his power to disobey even the law of his being. Selfishness is power without wisdom; it is energy wrongly directed. A man is selfish because he is ignorant of his nature and power as a mental being; such ignorance and selfishness entail suffering, and by repeated suffering and age-long experience he at last arrives at knowledge and the legitimate exercise of his power. The truly enlightened man cannot be selfish: he cannot accuse others of selfishness, or try to coerce them into being unselfish.

The selfish man is eager to bend others to his own way and will, believing it to be the only right way for all; he thereby ignorantly wastes himself in trying to check in others the power which he freely exercises himself, namely—the power to choose their own way and exercise their own will. By so doing, he places himself in direct antagonism with the like tendencies and freedom of other minds, and brings into operation the instruments of his own suffering. Hence the ceaseless inter-play of conflicting forces; the unending conflagration of passion; the turmoil, strife, and woe. Selfishness is misapplied power.

The unselfish man is he who, ceasing from all personal interference, abandoning the "I" as the source of judgment, and having recognized his illimitable freedom through the abandonment of all egotism even in thought, refrains from encroachment upon the boundless freedom of others, realizing the legitimacy of their choice and their right to the free employment of their power. However others may choose to act toward such a man, it can never cause him any trouble or suffering, because he is perfectly willing that they should so choose to act, and he harbors no wish that they should act in any other way. He realizes that his sole duty, as well as his entire power, *lies in acting rightly toward them*, and that he is in no way concerned with their actions toward him; that is both their choice and their business. To the unselfish man, therefore, malice, envy, backbiting, jealousy, accusation, condemnation, and persecution have passed away. Having ceased to practise these things, he is not disturbed when they are hurled at him. Thus liberation from sin is liberation from suffering. The selfless man is free; he has made the thraldom of sin impossible; he has broken every bond.

LIGHT ON THE BLESSING
AND DIGNITY OF WORK

That "labor is life" is a principle pregnant with truth, and one which cannot be too often repeated, or too closely studied and practised. Labor is so often regarded as an irksome and even degrading means of obtaining ease and pleasure, and not as what it really is—a thing happy and noble in itself, that the lesson contained in the maxim needs to be taken to heart and more and more thoroughly learned.

Activity, both mental and physical, is the essence of life. The complete cessation of activity is death, and death is immediately followed by corruption. Ease and death are closely associated. The more there is of activity, the more abounding is life. The brain-worker, the original thinker, the man of unceasing mental activity, is the longest-lived man in the community; the agricultural laborer, the gardener, the man of unceasing physical activity, comes next with length of years.

Pure-hearted, healthy-minded people love work, and are happy in their labors. They never complain of being "overworked." It is very difficult, almost impossible, for a man to be overworked if he lives a sound and pure life. It is worry, bad habits, discontent and idleness that kill—especially idleness, for if labor is life, then idleness must be death. Let us get rid of sin before we talk about being overworked.

There are those who are afraid of work, regarding it as an enemy, and who fear a breakdown by doing too much. They have to learn what a health-bestowing friend work is. Others are ashamed of work, looking upon it as a degrading thing to be avoided. The "pure in heart and sound in head" are neither afraid nor ashamed of work, and they dignify whatsoever they undertake. No necessary work can be degrading, but if a man regard his work as such, he is already degraded, not by his task, but by his slavish vanity.

> "Man hath his daily work of body and mind
> Appointed, which declares his dignity."

The idle man who is afraid of work, and the vain man who is ashamed of it, are both on the way to poverty, if they are not already there. The industrious man, who loves work, and the man of true dignity, who glorifies work, are both on their way to affluence, if they are not already there. The lazy man is sowing the seeds of poverty and crime; the vain man is sowing the seeds of humiliation and shame. The industrious man is sowing the seeds of affluence and virtue; the dignified worker is sowing the seeds of victory and honor. Deeds are seeds, and the harvest will appear in due season.

There is a common desire to acquire riches with as little effort as possible, which is a kind of theft. To try to obtain the fruits of labor without laboring is to take the fruits of another man's labor; to try to get money without giving its equivalent is to take that which belongs to another and not to one's self. What is theft but this frame of mind carried to its logical extreme?

Let us rejoice in our work; let us rejoice that we have the strength and capacity for work, and let us increase that strength and capacity by unremitting labor. Whatever our work may be, it is noble, and will be perceived by the world as noble, if we perform it in a noble spirit. The virtuous do not despise any labor which falls to their lot; and he who works and faints not, who is faithful, patient, and uncomplaining even in the time of poverty, he will surely at last eat of the sweet fruits of his labor; yea, even while he labors and seems to fail, happiness will be his constant companion, for, "Blessed is the man that has found his work; let him ask no other blessedness."

LIGHT ON GOOD MANNERS
AND REFINEMENT

"Move upward, working out the beast,
And let the ape and tiger die."

All culture is getting away from the beast. Evolution itself is a refining process, and the unwritten laws of society inhere in the evolutionary law.

Education is intellectual culture. The scholar is engaged in purifying and perfecting his intellect; the religious devotee is engaged in purifying and perfecting his heart.

When a man aspires to nobler heights of achievement, and sets about the realization of his ideal, he commences to refine his nature; and the more pure a man makes himself within, the more refined, gracious, and gentle will be his outward demeanor.

Good manners have an ethical basis, and cannot be divorced from religion. To be ill-mannered is to be imperfect, for what are ill manners but the outward expression of inward defects? What a man does, that he is. If he acts rudely he is a rude man; if he acts foolishly, he is a foolish man; if he acts gently, he is a gentleman. It is a mistake to suppose that a man can have a gentle and refined mind behind a rough and brutal exterior (though such a man may possess some strong animal virtues), as the outer is an expression of the inner.

One of the steps in the noble Eightfold Path to perfection as expounded by Buddha is—Right Conduct or Good Behavior, and it should be plain to all that the man who has not yet learned how to conduct himself toward others in a kindly, gracious, and unselfish spirit, has not yet entered the pathway of a holy life.

If a man refines his heart, he will refine his behavior; if he refines his behavior, it will help him to refine his heart.

To be coarse, brutish, and snappish may be natural to a beast, but the man who aspires to be even an endurable member of society (not to mention the higher manhood), will at once purge away any such bestial traits that may possess him.

All those things which aid in man's refinement—such as music, painting, poetry, manners—are servants and messengers of progress. Man degrades himself when he imitates the brute. Let us not mistake barbarism for simplicity, or vulgarity for honesty.

Unselfishness, kindliness, and consideration for others will always be manifested outwardly as gentleness, gra-

ciousness, and refinement. To affect these graces by simu-
lating them may seem to succeed, but it does not.
Affectation and hypocrisy are soon divulged; every man's
eye, sooner or later, pierces through their flimsiness, and
ultimately none but the actors of them are deceived. As
Emerson says:—

"What is done for effect, is seen to be done for effect;
and what is done for love, is felt to be done for love."

Children who are well-bred are taught always to consider the happiness of others before their own: to offer
them the most comfortable seat, the choicest fruit, the
best tidbit, and so on; and also to do everything, even the
most trivial acts, in the right way. And these two things—
unselfishness and right action—are at the basis, not only of
good manners, but of all ethics, religion, and true living:
they represent power and skill. The selfish man is weak and
unskilful in the exercise of thought; the vulgar man is
weak and unskilful in his actions. Unselfishness is the right
way of thinking; good manners are the right way of acting. As Emerson, again, says:—

"There is always a best way of doing everything, if it be
to boil an egg. Manners are the happy way of doing
things right."

It is a frequent error among men to imagine that the
Higher Life is an ideal something quite above and apart

from the common details of life, and that to neglect these or to perform them in a slovenly manner is an indication that the mind is occupied on "higher things." Whereas it is an indication that the mind is becoming inexact, dreamy, and weak, instead of exact, wide awake, and strong. No matter how apparently trivial the thing is which has to be done, there is a right way and a wrong way of doing it, and to do it in the right way saves friction, time, and trouble, conserves power, and develops grace, skill, and happiness.

The artisan has a variety of tools with which to ply his particular craft, and he is taught (and also finds by experience) that each tool must be applied to its special use, and never under any circumstances must one tool be made to do service for another. By using every tool in its proper place and in the right way, the maximum of dexterity and power is attained. Should a boy in learning a trade refuse instruction, and persist in using the tools in his own way, making one tool do service for another, he would never become anything better than a clumsy bungler, and would be a failure in his trade.

It is the same throughout the whole life. If a man opens himself to receive instruction, and studies how to do everything rightly and lawfully, he becomes strong and skilful and wise, master of himself, his thoughts and actions; but if he persists in following his momentary impulses, in doing everything as he feels prompted, not exercising thoughtfulness, and rejecting instruction, such a man will attain to nothing better than a slovenly and bungling life.

Confucius paid the strictest attention to dress, eating, deportment, passing speech—to all the so-called trivialities of life, as well as to the momentous affairs of state and the lofty moral principles which he expounded; and he taught his disciples that it is the sign of a vulgar and foolish mind to regard anything as "trivial" that is necessary to be done, that the wise man pays attention to all his duties, and does everything wisely, thoughtfully, and rightly.

It is not an arbitrary edict of society that the man who persists in eating with his knife shall be rejected, for a knife is given to cut with, and a fork to eat with, and to put things to wrong and slovenly uses—even in the passing details of life—does not make for progress, but is retrogressive and makes for confusion.

It is not a despotic condition in the law of things that so long as a man persists in thinking and acting unkindly of and toward others he shall be shut out from Heaven, and shall remain in the outer pain and unrest, for selfishness is disruption and disorder. The universe is sustained by exactness, it rests on order, it demands right doing, and the searcher for wisdom will watch all his ways. He will think purely, speak gently, and act graciously, refining his entire nature, both in the letter and the spirit.

LIGHT ON DIVERSITIES
OF CREEDS

Those who depart from the common track in matters of faith, and strike out independently in search of the Higher Life as distinguished from the letter of religious dogma, are apt to sink into a pitfall which awaits them at the first step, namely, the pitfall of *pride*. Attacking "creeds," and speaking contemptuously of "the orthodox" (as though orthodoxy were synonymous with evil) are not uncommon practices among those who fondly imagine they are in possession of greater spiritual light. Departure from orthodoxy does not by any means include departure from sin; indeed, it is not infrequently accompanied with increased bitterness and contempt. Change of opinion is one thing, change of heart is quite another. To withdraw one's adherence from creeds is easy; to withdraw one's self from sin is more difficult.

Hatred and pride, and not necessarily orthodoxy and

conformity, are the things to be avoided. One's own sin, and not another man's creed, is the thing to be despised. The right-minded man cannot plume himself on being "*broader*" than others, or assume that he is on a "higher plane" than others, or think with pharisaical contempt of those who still cling to some form of letter worship which he has abandoned. Applying the words "narrow," "big-oted," and "selfish" to others, is not the indication of an enlightened mind. No person would wish these terms to be applied to himself, and he who is becoming truly re-ligious, does not speak of others in words which would wound him were they directed toward himself.

Those who are learning how to exercise humility and compassion are becoming truly enlightened. Thinking lowly of themselves and kindly of others; condemning their own sins with merciless logic, and thinking with tender pity of the sins of others, they develop that insight into the nature and law of things which enables them to see the truth that is in others, and in the religions of oth-ers, and they do not condemn their neighbor because he holds a different faith, or because he adheres to a formal creed. Creeds must be, and he who performs faithfully his duty in his particular creed, not interfering with or con-demning his neighbor in the performance of his duty, is bringing the world nearer to perfection and peace.

Amid all the diversities of creeds there is the unifying power of undying and unalterable Love—and he who has Love has entered into sympathetic union with all.

He who has acquired the true spirit of Religion, who

has attained to pure insight and deep charity of heart, will avoid all strife and condemnation, and will not fall into the delusion of praising his own sect (should he belong to one) and trying to prove that it alone is right, and of dispraising other sects, and trying to prove that they are false. As the true man does not speak in praise of himself or his own work, so the man of humility, charity, and wisdom does not speak of his own sect as being superior to all others, nor seek to elevate his own particular religion by picking holes in forms of faith which are held as sacred by others.

Nothing more explicit and magnanimous has ever been uttered, in reference to this particular phase of the practice of charity, than is to be found in the twelfth Edict of Asoka, the great Indian Ruler and Saint who lived some two or three centuries previous to the Christian era, and whose life, devoted to the spread of Truth, testified to the beauty of his words: the edict runs thus:—

"There should be no praising of one's own sect and decrying of other sects; but, on the contrary, a rendering of honor to other sects for whatever cause honor may be due. By so doing, both one's own sect may be helped forward, and other sects will be benefited; by acting otherwise, one's own sect will be destroyed in injuring others. Whosoever exalts his own sect by decrying others, does so doubtless out of love for his own sect, thinking to spread abroad the fame thereof. But, on the contrary, he inflicts the more an injury upon his own sect."

These are wise and holy words; the breath of charity is in them, and they may be well pondered upon by those who are anxious to overthrow, not the religions of other men, but their own shortcomings.

It is a dark and deep-seated delusion that causes a man to think he can best advance the cause of his own religion by exposing what he regards as the "evils" of other religions; and the most pitiful part of it is, that while such a one rejoices in the thought that by continually belittling other sects he will perhaps at last wipe them out, and win all men to his side, he is all the time engaged in the sad work of bringing into disrepute, and thereby destroying, his own sect.

Just as every time a man slanders another, he inflicts lasting injury upon his own character and prospects, so every time one speaks evil of another sect, he soils and demeans his own. And the man who is prone to attack and condemn other religions is the one who suffers most when his own is attacked and condemned. If a man does not like that his own religion should be denounced as evil and false, he should carefully guard himself that he does not condemn other religions as such. If it pleases him when his own cause is well spoken of and helped, he should speak well of and help other causes which, while differing from his own in method, have the same good end in view. In this way he will escape the errors and miseries of sectarian strife, and will perfect himself in divine charity.

The heart that has embraced gentleness and charity

avoids all those blind passions which keep the fires of party strife, violence, persecution, and bitterness burning from age to age. It dwells in thoughts of pity and tenderness, scorning nothing, despising nothing, not stirring up enmity; for he who acquires gentleness, gains that clear insight into the Great Law which cannot be obtained in any other way, he sees that there is good in all sects and religions, and he makes that good his own.

Let the truth-seeker avoid divisions and invidious distinctions, and let him strive after charity; for charity does not slander, backbite, or condemn; it does not think of trampling down another's, and elevating its own.

Truth cannot contradict itself. The nature of Truth is exactness, reality, undeviating certitude. Why, then, the ceaseless conflict between the religions and creeds? Is it not because of error? Contradiction and conflict belong to the domain of error, for error, being confusion, is in the nature of self-contradiction. If the Christian says, "My religion is true and Buddhism is false," and if the Buddhist says, "Christianity is false and Buddhism is true," we are at once confronted with an irreconcilable contradiction, for these two religions cannot be both true and false. Such a contradiction cannot spring from Truth, and must therefore spring from error. But if both these religious partisans should now say, or think, "Yes, truly the contradiction springs from error, but the error is in the other man and his religion, and not in me and mine," this does but intensify the contradiction. Whence, then, springs the error, and where is Truth? Does not the very attitude of mind which these men adopt toward each other constitute the error? and were they to reverse that attitude, exchanging antagonism for good-will, would they not perceive the Truth which does not stand in conflict with itself?

The man who says, "My religion is true, and my neighbor's is false," has not yet discovered the truth in his own religion, for when a man has done that, he will see Truth in all religions. As behind all the universal phenomena there is but one Truth, so behind all the religions and creeds there is but one religion, for every religion contains the same ethical teaching, and all the Great Teachers taught exactly the same thing.

The precepts of the Sermon on the Mount are to be found in all religions, and the life which those precepts demand was lived by all the Great Teachers and many of their disciples, for the Truth is a pure heart and a blameless life, and not a set of dogmas and opinions. All religions teach purity of heart, holiness of life, compassion, love, and good-will; they teach the doing of good deeds and the giving up of selfishness and sin. These things are not dogmas, theologies, and opinions, they are things to be done, to be practised, to be lived. Men do not differ about these things, for they are the acknowledged verities in every sect. What, then, do they differ about? About their opinions, their speculations, their theologies.

Men differ about that which is unreal, not that which is real; they fight over error, and not over Truth. The very essential of all religion (and religions) is that before a man can know anything of Truth, he must cease from fighting his fellow-man, and shall learn to regard him with good-will and love; and how can a man do this while he is convinced that his neighbor's religion is false, and that it is his duty to do all that he can to undermine and overthrow it? This is not doing unto others as we would that they should do to us.

That which is true and real is true and real everywhere and always. There is no distinction between the pious Christian and the pious Buddhist. Purity of heart, piety of life, holy aspirations, and the love of Truth are the same in the Buddhist as the Christian. The good deeds of the Buddhist are not different from the good deeds of the Christian. Remorse for sin and sorrow for wrong thoughts and deeds spring in the hearts, not only of Christians, but men of all religions. Great is the need of sympathy. Great is the need of love.

All religions are the same in that they teach the same fundamental verities, but men, instead of practising these verities, engage in opinions and speculations about things which are outside the range of knowledge and experience, and it is in defending and promulgating their own particular speculations that men become divided and engage in conflict with each other.

Condemnation is incipient persecution. The thought, "I am right and you are wrong," is a seed prolific of hatred. It was out of this seed that the Spanish Inquisition grew. He who would find the universal Truth must abandon egotism, must quench the hateful flames of condemnation, and, taking out of his heart the baneful thought,

"All others are wrong," must think the illuminating thought, "It is I who am wrong," and having thus thought, he will cease from sin, and will live in love and good-will toward all, making no distinctions, engaging in no divisions, a peacemaker and not a partisan. Thus living charitably disposed toward all, he will become one with all, and will comprehend the Universal Truth, the Eternal Religion; for while error refutes error and selfishness divides, Truth demonstrates Truth and Religion unifies.

LIGHT ON LAW
AND MIRACLE

The love of the wonderful is an element in human nature, which, like passions and desires, requires to be curbed, directed, and finally transmuted; otherwise superstition and the obscuration of reason and insight cannot be avoided. The idea of miracle must be transcended before the orderly, eternal, and beneficent nature of law can be perceived, and that peace and certainty which a knowledge of law bestows can be enjoyed.

Just as a child when its eyes are opened to the phenomena of this world becomes involved in wonder, and revels in tales of giants and fairies, so when a man first opens his mental eyes to spiritual things does he become involved in stories of marvels and miracles; and as the child at last becomes a man and leaves behind him the crudities of childhood, understanding more accurately the relative nature of the phenomena around him, so with a fuller spiritual development and greater familiarity with the inner realities, a man at last leaves behind him the era of childish wonderment, comes into touch with the laws of things, and governs his life by principles that are fixed and invariable.

Law is universal and eternal, and, although vast areas of knowledge are waiting to be revealed, cause and effect will ever prevail, and every new discovery, every truth revealed, will serve to bring men nearer to a realization of the beauty, stability, and supremacy of law. And very gladdening it is to know that law is inviolable and eternal throughout every department of nature, for then we know that the operations of the universe are ever the same, and can therefore be discovered, understood, and obeyed. This is a ground of certainty, and therefore of great hope and joy. The idea of miracle is a denial of law and the substitution of an arbitrary and capricious power.

It is true that around the lives of the Great Teachers of humanity stories of miracle have grown, but they have emanated from the undeveloped minds of the people, and not from the Teachers themselves. Lao-Tze expounded the Supreme Law, or Reason, which admits of no miracle, yet his religion has, to-day, become so corrupted with the introduction of the marvellous as to be little better than a mass of superstition. Even Buddhism, whose founder declared that, "Seeing that the Law of Karma (cause and effect) governs all things, the disciple who aims at performing miracles does not understand the doctrine," and that "The desire to perform miracles arises either from covetousness or vanity," has surrounded, in its corrupted form, the life of its Great Master with a number of miracles. Even during the lifetime of Ramakrishna, the Hindu teacher who died in 1886, and who is regarded by his disciples as an incarnation of Deity to this age, all sorts of miracles were attributed to him by the people, and are now associated with his name; yet, according to Max Müller, these miracles are without any foundation of evidence or fact, and Ramakrishna himself ridiculed and repudiated miracle.

As men become more enlightened, miracles and wonder-working will be expunged from religion, and the orderly beauty of Law and the ethical grandeur of obedience to Law will become revealed and known. No man who desires to perform miracles or astral or psychological wonders, who is curious to see invisible or supernatural beings, or who is ambitious to become a "Master" or an "Adept," can attain a clear perception of Truth and the living of the highest life. Childish wonderment about things must be supplanted by knowledge of things, and vanity is a complete barrier to the entrance of the true path which demands of the disciple lowliness of heart, humility. He is on the true path who is cultivating kindliness, forbearance, and a loving heart; and the marks of the true Master are not miracles and wonder-working, but infinite patience, boundless compassion, spotless purity, and a heart at peace with all.

LIGHT ON WAR AND PEACE

War springs from inward strife. "War in heaven" precedes war on earth. When the inward spiritual harmony is destroyed by division and conflict, it will manifest itself outwardly in the form of war. Without this inward conflict war could not be, nor can war cease until the inward harmony is restored.

War consists of aggression and resistance, and after the fight has commenced both combatants are alike aggressors and resisters. Thus the effort to put an end to war by aggressive means produces war. "I have set myself stubbornly against the war spirit," said a man a short time ago. He did not know that he was, by that attitude of mind, practising and fostering the war spirit.

To fight against war is to produce war. It is impossible to fight for peace, because all fighting is the annihilation of peace. To think of putting an end to war by denouncing and fighting it is the same as if one should try to quench fire by throwing straw upon it. He, therefore, who is truly a man of peace, does not resist war, but practises peace. He who takes sides and practises attack and defence, is responsible for war, for he is always at war in his mind. He cannot know the nature of peace, for he has not arrived at peace in his own heart. The true man of peace is he who has put away from his mind the spirit of quarreling and party strife, who neither attacks others nor defends himself, and whose heart is at peace with all. Such a man has already laid in his heart the foundations of the empire of peace; he is a peace maker, for he is at peace with the whole world and practises the spirit of peace under all circumstances.

Very beautiful is the spirit of peace, and it says, "Come and rest." Bickerings, quarrellings, party divisions—these must be forever abandoned by him who would establish peace.

War will continue so long as men will allow themselves, individually, to be dominated by passion, and only when men have quelled the inward tumult will the outward horror pass away.

Self is the great enemy, the producer of all strife, and the maker of many sorrows; he, therefore, who will bring about peace on earth, let him overcome egotism, let him subdue his passions, let him conquer himself.

LIGHT ON THE BROTHERHOOD OF MAN

There is no lack of writing and preaching about "universal brotherhood," and it has been adopted as a leading article of faith by many newly formed societies; but what is so urgently needed to begin with, is not universal brotherhood, but *particular Brotherhood*, that is, the adoption of a magnanimous, charitable, and kindly spirit toward those with whom we come in immediate contact; toward those who contradict, oppose and attack us, as well as toward those who love and agree with us.

I make a very simple statement of truth when I say that until such particular brotherhood is practised, universal brotherhood will remain a meaningless term, for universal brotherhood is an end, a goal, and the way to it is by particular brotherhood; the one is a sublime and far-reaching consummation, the other is the means by which that consummation must be realized.

I remember on one occasion reading a paper devoted largely to the teaching of universal brotherhood, and the leading article—a long and learned one—was an exposition of this subject; but on turning over a few more pages, I found another piece by the same writer in which he accused of misrepresentation, lying, and selfishness, not his enemies, but the brethren of his own Society, who bear, at least as far as such sins are concerned, stainless reputations.

A scriptural writer has asked the question, "If a man love not his brother whom he hath seen, how can he love God whom he hath not seen?" In the same manner, if a man does not love the brother whom he knows, how can he love men of all creeds and all nations whom he does not know?

To write articles on universal brotherhood is one thing; to live in peace with one's relations and neighbors and to return good for evil is quite another.

To endeavor to propagate universal brotherhood while fostering in our heart some sparks of envy, spite, resentment, malice, or hatred, is to be self-deluded; for thus shall we be all the time hindering and denying, by our actions, that which we eulogize by our words; but so subtle is such self-delusion, that, until the very heights of love and wisdom are reached, we are all liable at any moment to fall into it.

It is not because our fellow-men do not hold our views, or follow our religion, or see as we see, that universal brotherhood remains unrealized, but because of the prevalence of ill-will; and if we hate, avoid, and condemn others because they differ from us, or treat selfishly and harshly those who are near to us, all that we may say or do in the cause of universal brotherhood will be only another snare to our feet, a mockery to our aspirations, and a farce to the world at large.

Let us, then, remove all hatred and malice from our hearts; let us be filled with good-will toward those who try and test us by their immediate nearness; let us love them that hate us, and think magnanimously of those who condemn us or our doctrine—in a word, let us take the first step toward universal brotherhood, by practising brotherhood in the place where we now are, and toward those with whom we associate, which is the place where it is most needed; and as we succeed in being brotherly in these important particulars, universal brotherhood will be found to be not far distant.

LIGHT ON LIFE'S SORROWS

There is great sorrow in the world. This is one of the supreme facts of life. Grief and affliction visit every heart, and many that are to-day revelling in hilarious joy or sinful riot, will to-morrow be smitten low with sorrow. Suddenly, and with swift and silent certainty, comes its poignant arrow, entering the human heart, slaying its joy, laying low its hopes, and shattering all its earthly plans and prospects. Then the humbled, smitten soul reflects, and enters deeply and sympathetically into the hidden meanings of human life.

In the dark times of sorrow, men approach very near to Truth. When in one brief hour the builded hopes of many years of toil fall like a toy palace, and all earthly pleasures burst and vanish like petty bubbles in the grasp, then the crushed spirit, bewildered, tempest-tossed, and without a refuge, gropes in dumb anguish for the Eternal, and seeks its abiding peace.

"Blessed are they that mourn," said the Teacher of the West, and the Teacher of the East declared that "Where there is great suffering there is great bliss." Both these sayings express the truth that sorrow is a teacher and a purifier. Sorrow is not the end of life—though it is, in its consummation, the end of the worldly life—but it is the beginning of the heavenly life; it leads the bewildered spirit into rest and safety; for the end of sorrow is joy and peace.

Strong searcher for Truth! Strenuous fighter against self and passion! seasons of sorrow must be your portion for a time. While any vestige of self remains, temptations will assail you, and the veil of illusion will cloud your spiritual vision, producing sorrow and unrest; and when heavy clouds settle down upon your spirit, accept the darkness as your own, and pass through it bravely into the cloudless light beyond.

Bear well in mind that nothing can overtake you that does not belong to you and that is not for your eternal good. As the poet has truly sung—

"Nor space nor time, nor deep nor high Can keep my own away from me."

And not alone are the bright things of life yours; the dark things are yours also. When difficulties and troubles gather thickly about you; when failures come and friends fall away; when the tongue that sweetly praised you, bitterly blames; when beloved lips that pressed upon your lips the soft, warm kisses of love, taunt and mock you in the lonely hour of your solitary grief; or when you lay beneath the sod the cold casket of clay that but yesterday held the responsive spirit of your beloved,—when these things overtake you, remember that the hour of your Gethsemane has come, that the cup of anguish is yours to drink. Drink it silently and murmur not, for in that hour of oppressive darkness and blinding pain no prayer will save you, no cry to heaven will bring you sweet relief; but faith and patience only will give you the strength to endure, and to go through your crucifixion with a meek and gentle spirit, not complaining, blaming no one, but accepting it as your own.

When one has reached the lowest point of sorrow; when, weak and exhausted, and overcome with a sense of powerlessness, he cries to God for help, and there comes no answering comfort and no succor—then, discovering the painfulness of sorrow and the insufficiency of prayer alone, he is ready to enter the path of self-renunciation, ready to purify his heart, ready to practise self-control, ready to become a spiritual athlete, and to develop that divine and invincible strength which is born of self-mastery.

He will find the cause of sorrow in his own heart, and will remove it. He will learn to stand alone; not craving sympathy from any, but giving it to all. Not thoughtlessly sinning and remorsefully repenting, but studying how not to commit sin. Humbled by innumerable defeats, and chastened by many sufferings, he will learn how to act blamelessly toward others, how to be gently and strong, kind and steadfast, compassionate and wise.

Thus he will gradually rise above sorrow, and at last Truth will dawn upon his mind, and he will understand the meaning of abiding peace. His mental eye will open to perceive the Cosmic Order. He will be blessed with the Vision of the Law, and will receive the Beatific Bliss.

When the true order of things is perceived, sorrow is transcended. When the contracted personal self which hugs its own little fleeting pleasures and broods over its own petty disappointments and dissatisfactions is broken up and cast away, then the larger life of Truth enters the mind, bringing bliss and peace; and the Universal Will takes the place of self. The individual becomes one with humanity. He forgets self in his love for all. His sorrow is swallowed up in the bliss of Truth.

Thus when you have, by experience, entered completely into the sorrow that is never lifted from the heart of mankind; when you have reaped and eaten all the bitter fruits of your own wrong thoughts and deeds—then divine compassion for all suffering beings will be born in your heart, healing all your wounds and drying all your tears. You will rise again into a new and heavenly life, where the sting of sorrow cannot enter, for there is no self there. After the crucifixion comes the transfiguration; the sorrowless state is reached through sorrow, and "the wise do not grieve."

Ever remember this—in the midst of sin and sorrow there abides the world of Truth. Redemption is at hand. The troubled may find peace; the impure may find purity. Healing awaits the broken-hearted; the weak will be adorned with strength, and the downtrodden will be lifted up and glorified.

LIGHT ON LIFE'S CHANGES

The tendency of things to advance from a lower to a higher level, and from high to higher still, is universal. The worlds exist in order that beings may experience, and by experiencing, acquire knowledge and increase in wisdom.

Evolution is only another word for progress. It signifies perpetual change, but a purposeful change, a change accompanied by growth. Evolution does not mean the creation of a new being from a being of a different order; it means the modification of beings by experience and change; and such modification is progress.

The fact of change is ever before us. Nothing can escape it. Plants, animals, and men germinate, reach maturity, and pass into decay. Even the lordly suns and their attendant worlds rolling through illimitable spaces, although their life is reckoned in millions of years, at last

JAMES ALLEN

decay and perish after having passed through innumerable changes. We cannot say of any being or object—"This will remain forever as it is," for even while we are saying it, the being or object would be undergoing change.

Sadness and suffering accompany this change; and beings mourn for that which has departed, for the things which are lost and gone. Yet in reality change is good, for it is the open door to all achievement, advancement and perfection.

Mind, as well as matter, is subject to the same change. Every experience, every thought, every deed, changes a man. There is little resemblance between the old man and his period of childhood and youth.

An eternally fixed, unchangeable being is not known. Such a being may be assumed, but it is a postulate only. It is not within the range of human observation and knowledge. A being not subject to change would be a being outside progress.

There is a teaching which declares that man has a spiritual soul that is eternally pure, eternally unchanged, eternally perfect, and that the sinning, suffering, changing man as we see him is an illusion—that, indeed, the spiritual soul is *the* man, and the other is an unreality.

There is another teaching that affirms that man is eternally imperfect, that stainless purity can never be reached, and that perfection is an impossibility, an illusion.

It will be found that these two extremes have no relation to *human experience*. They are both of the nature of

200

speculative metaphysics which stand in opposition to the *facts of life*; so much so that the adherents of these two extremes deny the existence of the commonest every-day facts of human experience. That which is assumed is regarded as real; the facts of life are declared to be unreal.

It is well to avoid both these extremes, and find the middle way of human experience. It is well to avoid opinions and speculations of our own or others, it is well to *refer to the facts of life*. We see that man passes through birth and growth and old age, that he experiences sin, sickness, and death; that he sorrows and suffers, aspires and rejoices; and that he is ever looking forward to greater purity and striving toward perfection. These are not opinions, speculations, or metaphysics—they are universal facts.

If man were already perfect, there were no need for him to be perfected, and all moral teaching would be useless and ridiculous. Moreover, a perfect being could not be subject to illusion and unreality.

On the other hand, if a man could never attain to purity and perfection, his aspirations and strivings would be useless. They would indeed be mockeries; and the heavenly perfection of saintly and divine men would have to be belittled and denied.

We see around us sin and sorrow and suffering; and we see before us, in the lives of the great teachers, the sinless, sorrowless, divine state. Therefore, we know that man is an imperfect being, yet capable of, and destined for, perfection. The divine state toward which he aspires, he will reach. The fact that he so ardently desires it, means that he can reach it, even if the fact were not demonstrated in those great ones who have already attained.

Man is not a compound of two beings, one real and perfect, the other unreal and imperfect. He is one and real, and his experiences are real. His imperfection is apparent, and his advancement and progress are also apparent.

The realities of life claim men in spite of their metaphysics, and all come under the same law of change and progress. He who affirms the eternal sinlessness and perfection of man, should not, to be logical and consistent, ever speak of sins and faults, of disease and death; yet he refers to these things as matters to be dealt with. Thus in theory he denies the existence of that which he habitually recognizes in practice.

He also who denies the possibility of perfection, should not aspire or strive; yet we find him practising self-denial and striving ceaselessly toward perfection.

Holding to the theoretical does not absolve men from the inevitable. The teacher of the unreality of sickness, old age, and death is at last caught in the toils of disease, succumbs to age, and disappears in death.

Change is not only inevitable, it is constant and unvarying law. Without it, everything would remain forever as it is, and there could be neither growth nor progress.

The strenuous struggle of all life is a prophecy of its perfection. The lookings upward of all beings is evidence of their ceaseless ascension. Aspirations, ideals, moral aims, while they denote man's imperfection, assuredly point to his future perfection. They are neither unnecessary nor aimless, but are woven into the fabric of things; they belong to the vital essence of the universe.

Whatsoever a man believes or disbelieves, what theories he holds or does not hold, one thing is certain—he is found in the stream of life, and *must* think and act; and to think and act is to experience; and to experience is to change and develop.

That man is conscious of sin, means that he can become pure; that he abhors evil, signifies that he can reach up to Good; that he is a pilgrim in the land of error, assures us, without doubt, that he will at last come to the beautiful city of Truth.

LIGHT ON THE TRUTH
OF TRANSITORINESS

I t is well sometimes to meditate deeply and seriously on the truth of Transitoriness. By meditation we will come to perceive how all compounded things must pass away; yea, how even while they remain they are already in process of passing away. Such meditation will soften the heart, deepen the understanding, and render one more fully conscious of the sacred nature of life.

What is there that does not pass away, among all the things of which a man says, "This will be mine tomorrow"? Even the mind is continually changing. Old characteristics die and pass away, and new ones are formed. In the midst of life all things are dying. Nothing endures; nothing can be retained. Things appear and then disappear; they become, and then they pass away.

The ancient sages declared the visible universe to be

Mâyâ, illusion, meaning thereby that impermanency is the antithesis of Reality. Change and decay are in the very nature of visible things, and they are unreal—illusory—in the sense that they pass away forever.

He who would ascend into the realm of Reality, who would penetrate into the world of Truth, must first perceive, with no uncertain vision, the transitory nature of the things of life; he must cease to delude himself into believing that he can retain his hold on his possessions, his body, his pleasures and objects of pleasure; for as the flower fades and as the leaves of the tree fall and wither, so must these things, in their season, pass away for ever.

The perception of the Truth of Transitoriness is one of the first great steps in wisdom, for when it is fully grasped, and its lesson has sunk deeply into the heart, the clinging to perishable things which is the cause of all sorrow, will be yielded up, and the search for the Truth which abides will be accelerated.

Anguish is rife because men set their hearts on the acquisition of things that perish, because they lust for the possession of those things which even when obtained cannot be retained.

There is no sorrow that would not vanish if the clinging to evanescent things were given up; there is no grief that would not be dispersed if the desire to have and to hold those things which in their very nature cannot endure, were taken out of the heart.

Tens of thousands of grief-stricken hearts are to-day

bewailing the loss of some loved object which they called theirs in days that are past, are weeping over that which is gone forever and cannot be restored.

Men are slow to learn the lessons of experience and to acquire wisdom, and unnumbered griefs and pains and sorrows have failed to impress them with the Truth of Transitoriness. He who clings to that which is impermanent, cannot escape sorrow, and the intensity of his sorrow will be measured by the strength of his clinging. He who sets his heart on perishable things embraces the companionship of grief and lamentation.

Men cannot find wisdom because they will not renounce the clinging to things, because they believe that the clinging to perishable objects is the source of happiness, and not the cause of sorrow; they cannot escape unrest and enter into the life of peace because desire is difficult to quench, and the immediate and transitory pleasure which gratified desire affords is mistaken for abiding joy.

It is because the true order of things is not understood that grief is universal; it is ignorance of the fleeting nature of things that lies at the root of sorrow.

The sting of anguish will be taken out of life when the lust to hold and to preserve the things of decay is taken out of the heart.

Sorrow is ended for him who sees things as they are; who, realizing the nature of transiency, detaches his heart and mind from the things that perish.

There is a right use for perishable things, and when

they are rightly used, and not doted upon for themselves alone, their loss will cause no sorrow.

If a rich man thinks in his heart, "My riches and possessions are no part of me, nor can I call them mine, seeing that when I am summoned to depart from this world, I cannot take them with me; they are entrusted to me to use rightly, and I will employ them to the best of my ability for the good of men and for the world," such a man, though surrounded by luxuries and responsibilities, will be lifted above sorrow, and will draw near to Truth. On the other hand, if the poor man does not covet riches and possessions, his condition will cause him no anxiety and unrest.

He who by a right understanding of life rids his heart of all selfish grasping and clinging, who uses everything wisely and in its proper place, and who, with chastened heart, and mind clarified of all thirsty desires, remains serene and self-contained in the midst of all changes, such a man will find Truth, he will stand face to face with Reality.

For in the midst of all error there abides the Truth; at the heart of transiency there reposes the Permanent; and illusion does but veil the eternal and unchanging Reality.

The nature of that Reality it is not my purpose to deal with here; let it suffice that I indicate that it is only found by abandoning, in the heart, all that is not of Love and Compassion and Wisdom and Purity. In these things there is no element of transitoriness, no sorrow, and no unrest.

When the truth of Transitoriness is well perceived, and

when the lesson contained in the truth of Transitoriness is well learned, then does a man set out to find the abiding Truth; then does he wean his heart from those selfish elements which are productive of sorrow.

He whose treasure is Truth, who fashions his life in accordance with Wisdom, will find the Joy which does not pass away, will leave behind him the land of lamentation, and, crossing the wide ocean of illusion, will come to the Sorrowless Shore.

THE LIGHT THAT NEVER
GOES OUT

Amid the multitude of conflicting opinions and theories, and caught in the struggle of existence, whither shall the confused truthseeker turn to find the path that leads to peace unending? To what refuge shall he fly from the uncertainties and sorrows of change?

Will he find peace in pleasure? Pleasure has its place, and in its place it is good; but as an end, as a refuge, it affords no shelter, and he who seeks it as such does but increase the anguish of life; for what is more fleeting than pleasure, and what is more empty than the heart that seeks satisfaction in so ephemeral a thing? There is, therefore, no abiding refuge in pleasure.

Will he find peace in wealth and worldly success? Wealth and worldly success have their place, but they are fickle and uncertain possessions, and he who seeks them for themselves alone will be burdened with many anxieties and cares; and when the storms of adversity sweep over his glittering yet frail habitation, he will find himself helpless and exposed. But even should he maintain such possessions throughout life, what satisfaction will they afford him in the hour of death? There is no abiding refuge in wealth and worldly success.

Will he find peace in health? Health has its place, and it should not be thrown away or despised, but it belongs to the body which is destined for dissolution, and is therefore perishable. Even should health be maintained for a hundred years, the time will come when the physical energies will decline and debility and decay will overtake them. There is no abiding refuge in health.

Will he find refuge in those whom he dearly loves? Those whom he loves have their place in his life. They afford him means of practising unselfishness, and therefore of arriving at Truth. He should cherish them with loving care, and consider their needs before his own; but the time will come when they will be separated from him, and he will be left alone. There is no abiding refuge in loved ones.

Will he find peace in this Scripture or that? Scripture fills an important place. As a guide it is good, but it cannot be a refuge, for one may know the Scripture by heart, and yet be in sore conflict and unrest. The theories of men are subject to successive changes, and no limit can be set to the variety of textual interpretations. There is no abiding refuge in Scripture.

Will he find rest in this teacher or that? The teacher has his place, and as an instructor he renders good service. But teachers are numerous, and their differences are many; though one may regard his particular teacher as in possession of Truth, that teacher will one day be taken from him. There is no abiding refuge in a teacher.

Will he find peace in solitude? Solitude is good and necessary in its place, but he who courts it as a lasting refuge will be like one perishing of thirst in a waterless desert. He will escape men and the turmoil of the city, but he will not escape himself and the unrest of his heart. There is no abiding rest in solitude.

If, then, the seeker can find no refuge in pleasure, in success, in health, in friends, in Scripture, in the teacher, or in solitude, whither shall he turn to find that sanctuary which shall afford abiding peace?

Let him take refuge in righteousness; let him fly to the sanctuary of a purified heart. Let him enter the pathway of a blameless, stainless life, and walk it meekly and patiently until it brings him to the eternal temple of Truth in his own heart.

He who has taken refuge in Truth, even in the habitation of a wise understanding and a loving and steadfast heart, is the same whether in pleasure or pain; wealth or poverty; success or failure; health or sickness; with friends or without; in solitude or noisy haunts; and he is independent of bibles and teachers, for the Spirit of Truth instructs him. He perceives, without fear or sorrow, the change and decay which are in all things. He has found peace; he has entered the abiding sanctuary; he knows the Light that will never go out.

WHAT YOU CAN DO WITH YOUR WILL POWER

Russell H. Conwell

PREFACE

Other writers have fully and accurately described *the road*, and my only hope is that these hastily written lines will inspire the young man or young woman to arise *and go*.

RUSSELL H. CONWELL

WHAT YOU CAN DO WITH
YOUR WILL POWER

I

Success has no secret. Her voice is forever ringing through the market-place and crying in the wilderness, and the burden of her cry is one word—WILL. Any normal young man who hears and heeds that cry is equipped fully to climb to the very heights of life.

The message I would like to leave with the young men and women of America is a message I have been trying humbly to deliver from lecture platform and pulpit for more than fifty years. It is a message the accuracy of which has been affirmed and reaffirmed in thousands of lives whose progress I have been privileged to watch. And the message is this: Your future stands before you like a block

The Author is much indebted to Mr. Merle Crowell of the *American Magazine* who assisted most efficiently in the preparation of the facts herein contained.

of unwrought marble. You can work it into what you will. Neither heredity, nor environment, nor any obstacles superimposed by man can keep you from marching straight through to success, provided you are guided by a firm, driving determination and have normal health and intelligence.

Determination is the battery that commands every road of life. It is the armor against which the missiles of adversity rattle harmlessly. If there is one thing I have tried peculiarly to do through these years it is to indent in the minds of the youth of America the living fact that when they give WILL the reins and say "DRIVE" they are headed toward the heights.

The institution out of which Temple University, of Philadelphia, grew was founded thirty years ago expressly to furnish opportunities for higher education to poor boys and girls who are willing to work for it. I have seen ninety thousand students enter its doors. A very large percentage of these came to Philadelphia without money, but firmly determined to get an education. I have never known one of them to go back defeated. Determination has the properties of a powerful acid; all shackles melt before it.

Conversely, lack of will power is the readiest weapon in the arsenal of failure. The most hopeless proposition in the world is the fellow who thinks that success is a door through which he will sometime stumble if he roams around long enough. Some men seem to expect ravens to feed them, the cruse of oil to remain inexhaustible, the fish to come right up over the side of the boat at meal-time.

They believe that life is a series of miracles. They loaf about and trust in their lucky star, and boldly declare that the world owes them a living.

As a matter of fact the world owes a man nothing that he does not earn. In this life a man gets about what he is worth, and he must render an equivalent for what is given him. There is no such thing as inactive success.

My mind is running back over the stories of thousands of boys and girls I have known and known about, who have faced every sort of a handicap and have won out solely by will and perseverance in working with all the power that God had given them. It is now nearly thirty years since a young English boy came into my office. He wanted to attend the evening classes at our university to learn oratory.

"Why don't you go into the law?" I asked him.

"I'm too poor! I haven't a chance!" he replied, shaking his head sadly.

I turned on him sharply. "Of course you haven't a chance," I exclaimed, "if you don't make up your mind to it!"

The next night he knocked at my door again. His face was radiant and there was a light of determination in his eyes.

"I have decided to become a lawyer," he said, and I knew from the ring of his voice that he meant it.

Many times after he became mayor of Philadelphia he must have looked back on that decision as the turning-point in his life.

I am thinking of a young Connecticut farm lad who was given up by his teachers as too weak-minded to learn. He left school when he was seven years old and toiled on his father's farm until he was twenty-one. Then something turned his mind toward the origin and development of the animal kingdom. He began to read works on zoology, and, in order to enlarge his capacity for understanding, went back to school and picked up where he left off fourteen years before. Somebody said to him, "You can get to the top *if you will!*"

He grasped the hope and nurtured it, until at last it completely possessed him. He entered college at twenty-eight and worked his way through with the assistance that we were able to furnish him. To-day he is a respected professor of zoology in an Ohio college.

Such illustrations I could multiply indefinitely. Of all the boys whom I have tried to help through college I cannot think of a single one who has failed for any other reason than ill health. But of course I have never helped any one who was not first helping himself. As soon as a man determines the goal toward which he is marching, he is in a strategic position to see and seize everything that will contribute toward that end.

Whenever a young man tells me that if he "had his way" he would be a lawyer, or an engineer, or what not, I always reply:

"You can be what you will, provided that it is something the world will be demanding ten years hence."

This brings to my mind a certain stipulation which

the ambition of youth must recognize. You must invest yourself or your money in a *known demand*. You must select an occupation that is fitted to your own special genius and to some actual want of the people. Choose as early as possible what your life-work will be. Then you can be continually equipping yourself by reading and observing to a purpose. There are many things which the average boy or girl learns in school that could be learned outside just as well.

Almost any man should be able to become wealthy in this land of opulent opportunity. There are some people who think that to be pious they must be very poor and very dirty. They are wrong. Not money, but the *love* of money, is the root of all evil. Money in itself is a dynamic force for helping humanity.

In my lectures I have borne heavily on the fact that we are all walking over acres of diamonds and mines of gold. There are people who think that their fortune lies in some far country. It is much more likely to lie right in their own back yards or on their front door-step, hidden from their unseeing eye. Most of our millionaires discovered their fortunes by simply looking around them.

Recently I have been investigating the lives of four thousand and forty-three American millionaires. All but twenty of them started life as poor boys, and all but forty of them have contributed largely to their communities, and divided fairly with their employees as they went along. But, alas, not one rich man's son out of seventeen dies rich.

But if a man has dilly-dallied through a certain space of wasted years, can he then develop the character—the motor force—to drive him to success? Why, my friend, will power cannot only be developed, but it is often dry powder which needs only a match. Very frequently I think of the life of Abraham Lincoln—that wonderful man! and I am thankful that I was permitted to meet him. Yet Abraham Lincoln developed the splendid sinews of his will after he was twenty-one. Before that he was just a roving, goodnatured sort of a chap. Always have I regretted that I failed to ask him what special circumstance broke the chrysalis of his life and loosened the wings of his will.

Many years ago some of the students of Temple University held a meeting in a building opposite the Bellevue-Stratford Hotel. As they were leaving the building they noticed a foreigner selling peanuts on the opposite curb. While buying peanuts they got to talking with the fellow, and told him that any one could obtain an education if he was willing to work for it. Eagerly the poor fellow drank up all the information he could get. He enrolled at Temple University and worked his way through, starting with the elementary studies. He is to-day an eminent practising physician in the national capital.

Often I think of an office clerk who reached a decision that the ambitions which were stirring in his soul could be realized if he could only get an education. He attended our evening classes and was graduated with a B.S. degree. He is now the millionaire head of one of the largest brokerage houses in the country.

"Where there's a will there's a way!" But one needs to use a little common sense about selecting the way. A general may determine to win a victory, but if he hurls his troops across an open field straight into the leaden sweep of the enemy's artillery he invites disaster and defeat. The best general lays his plans carefully, and advances his troops in the way that will best conserve their strength and numbers. So must a man plan his campaign of life.

No man has a right, either for himself or for others, to be at work in a factory, or a store, or anywhere else, unless he would work there from choice—money or no money—if he had the necessities of life.

"As a man thinks, so he is," says the writer of Proverbs; but as a man adjusts himself, so really is he, after all. One great trouble with many individuals is that they are made up of all sorts of machinery that is not adjusted, that is out of place—no belts on the wheels, no fire under the boiler, hence no steam to move the mechanism.

Some folk never take the trouble to size themselves up—to find out what they are fitted to do—and then wonder why they remain way down at the bottom of the heap. I remember a young woman who told me that she did not believe she could ever be of any particular use in the world. I mentioned a dozen things that she ought to be able to do.

"If you only knew yourself," I said, "you would set yourself to writing. You ought to be an author."

She shook her head and smiled, as if she thought I was making fun of her. Later, force of circumstances drove her to take up the pen. And when she came to me and told me that she was making three thousand dollars a year in literary work, and was soon to go higher, I thought back to the time when she was a poor girl making three dollars a week when she failed accurately to estimate herself.

II

There is a deplorable tendency among many people to wait for a particularly favorable opportunity to declare themselves in the battle of life. Some people pause for the rap of opportunity when opportunity has been playing a tattoo on their resonant skulls for years.

Hardly a single great invention has been placed on the market without a number of men putting forth the claim that they had the idea first—and in most cases they proved the fact. But while they were sitting down and dreaming, or trying to bring the device to a greater perfection, a man with initiative rose up and acted. The telegraph, telephone, sewing-machine, air-brake, mowing-machine, wireless, and linotype-machine are only a few illustrations.

The most wonderful idea is quite valueless until it is put into practical operation. The Government rewards the man who first gets a patent or first puts his invention into practical use—and the world does likewise. Thus the dreamer must always lag behind the door.

True will power also predicates concentration. I shall never forget the time I went to see President Lincoln to ask him to spare the life of one of my soldiers who was sentenced to be shot. As I walked toward the door of his office I felt a greater fear than I had ever known when the shells were bursting all about us at Antietam. Finally I mustered up courage to knock on the door. I heard a voice inside yell:

"Come in and sit down!"

The man at the table did not look up as I entered; he was busy over a bunch of papers. I sat down at the edge of a chair and wished I were in Peking or Patagonia. He never looked up until he had quite finished with the papers. Then he turned to me and said:

"I am a very busy man and have only a few minutes to spare. Tell me in the fewest words what it is you want."

As soon as I mentioned the case he said:

"I have heard all about it, and you do not need to tell me any more. Mr. Stanton was talking to me about that only a few days ago. You can go to the hotel and rest assured that the President never did sign an order to shoot a boy under twenty, and never will. You may tell his mother that." Then, after a short conversation, he took hold of another bunch of papers and said, decidedly, "Good morning!"

Lincoln, one of the greatest men of the world, owed his success largely to one rule: whatsoever he had to do at all he put his whole mind into, and held it all there until the task was all done. That makes men great almost anywhere.

Too many people are satisfied if they have done a thing "well enough." That is a fatal complacency. "Well enough" has cursed souls. "Well enough" has wrecked enterprises. "Well enough" has destroyed nations. If perfection in a task can possibly be reached, nothing short of perfection is "well enough." Governor Talbot of Massachusetts got his high office because General Swift made a happy application of the truth in saying to the convention, "I nominate for Governor of this state a man who, when he was a farmer's boy, hoed to the end of the row." That saying became a campaign slogan all up and down the state. "He hoed to the end of the row! He hoed to the end of the row!" When the people discovered that this was one of the characteristics of the man, they elected him by one of the greatest majorities ever given a Governor in Massachusetts.

Yet we must bear in mind that there is such a thing as overdoing anything. Young people should draw a line between study that secures wisdom and study that breaks down the mind; between exercise that is healthful and exercise that is injurious; between a conscientiousness that is pure and divine and a conscientiousness that is over-morbid and insane; between economy that is careful and economy that is stingy; between industry that is a reasonable use of their powers and industry that is an over-use of their powers, leading only to destruction.

The best ordered mind is one that can grasp the problems that gather around a man constantly and work them out to a logical conclusion; that sees quickly what anything means, whether it be an exhibition of goods, a juxtaposition of events, or the suggestions of literature.

A man is made up largely of his daily observations.

School training serves to fit and discipline him so that he may read rightly the lesson of the things he sees around him. Men have made mighty fortunes by just using their eyes.

Several years ago I took dinner in New York with one of the great millionaires of that city. In the course of our talk he told me something about his boyhood days—how, with hardly a penny in his pocket, he slung a pack on his back and set out along the Erie Canal, looking for a job. At last he got one. He was paid three dollars a week to make soft soap for the laborers to use at the locks in washing their hands. One can hardly imagine a more humble occupation; but this boy kept his eyes open. He saw the disadvantages of soft soap, and set to work to make a hard substitute for it. Finally he succeeded, and his success brought him many, many millions.

Every person is designed for a definite work in life, fitted for a particular sphere. Before God he has a right to that sphere. If you are an excellent housekeeper you should not be running a loom, and it is your duty to prepare yourself to enter at the first opportunity the sphere for which you are fitted.

George W. Childs, who owned the Philadelphia *Ledger*, once blacked boots and sold newspapers in front of the *Ledger* building. He told me how he used to look at that building and declare over and over to himself that some day he would own the great newspaper establishment that it housed. When he mentioned his ambition to his associates they laughed at him. But Childs had indomitable grit, and ultimately he did come to own that newspaper establishment, one of the finest in the country.

Another thing very necessary to the pursuit of success is the proper employment of waiting moments. How do you use your waiting time for meals, for trains, for business? I suppose that if the average individual were to employ wisely these intervals in which he whistles and twiddles his thumbs he would soon accumulate enough knowledge to quite make over his life.

I went through the United States Senate in 1867 and asked each of the members how he got his early education. I found that an extremely large percentage of them had simply properly applied their waiting moments. Even Charles Sumner, a university graduate, told me that he learned more from the books he read outside of college than from those he had studied within. General Burnside, who was then a Senator, said that he had always had a book beside him in the shop where he worked.

Before leaving the subject of the power of the will, there is one thing I would like to say: a true will must have a decent regard for the happiness of others. Do not get so wrapped up in your own mission that you forget to be kind to other people, for you have not fulfilled every duty unless you have fulfilled the duty of being pleasant. Enemies and ignorance are the two most expensive things in a man's life. I never make unnecessary enemies—they cost too much.

Every one has within himself the tools necessary to carve out success. Consecrate yourself to some definite mission in life, and let it be a mission that will benefit the world as well as yourself. Remember that nothing can withstand the sweep of a determined will—unless it happens to be another will equally as determined. Keep clean, fight hard, pick your openings judiciously, and have your eyes forever fixed on the heights toward which you are headed. If there be any other formula for success, I do not know it.

III

The biography of that great patriot and statesman, Daniel Manin of Venice, Italy, contains a very romantic example of the possibilities of will force. He was born in a poor quarter of the city; his parents were without rank or money. Venice in 1805 was under the Austrian rule and was sharply divided into aristocratic and peasant classes. He was soon deserted by his father and left to the support of his mother. He was a dull boy, and could not keep along with other boys in the church schools; his mind labored as slowly as did the childhood intellects of many of the greatest men of history. Daniel seemed destined to earn his living digging mud out of the canals, if he supported himself at all. No American boy can be handicapped like that. But the children who learn slowly learn surely, and history, which is but the biography of great men, mentions again and again the fact that the great characters began to be able to acquire learning late in life. Napoleon and Wellington were both dull boys, and

Lincoln often said that he was a dunce through his early years. Daniel Manin seems to have been utterly unable to learn from books until he was eight or ten years old. But his latent will power was suddenly developed to an unexpected degree when he was quite a youth. Kossuth, who was a personal friend of Manin, said in an address in New York that the American Republic was responsible for the awakening of Manin, and through him had made Italy free.

It appears that an American sea-captain, while discharging a cargo in Venice, employed Daniel as an errand-boy, and when the ship sailed the captain made Daniel a present of a gilt-edged copy of the lives of George Washington and John Hancock in one volume. The captain, who had greatly endeared himself to Daniel, made the boy promise solemnly that he would learn to read the book. But Daniel was utterly ignorant of the English language in print and had learned only a few phrases from the captain. The gift of that book made Venice a republic, led to the adoption of sections of the United States Constitution by that state and carried the principles on into the constitution of United Italy. That book awakened the sleeping will power of the industrious dull boy. Even his mother protested against his waste of time in trying to read English when he was unable to conquer the primers in Italian. But he secured a phrase-book and a grammar, and paid for them in hard labor. With those crude implements, without a teacher, he determined to read that book. Only one friend, a young priest in St. Mark's

Cathedral, gave him any word or look of encouragement. But his candle burned late, and the returning daylight took him to his book to study until time for breakfast. Then came the daily task as a messenger, or gondolier. Some weeks or months after he began his seemingly foolish problem he rushed into his mother's room at night, excited and noisy, shouting to her: "I can read that book! I can read that book!" There comes a moment in the life of every successful student of a foreign language when he suddenly awakens to the consciousness that he can think in that language. From that point on the work is always easy. It must have been a similar psychological change which came into Daniel's intellect. So sudden was it, so amazing the change, that the priest reported the case as a miracle, and the little circle of the poor people who knew the boy looked on him with awe. Consul—General Sparks, who represented the United States at Venice in 1848, wrote that "Manin often mentions his intellectual new birth, and his success in reading the life of Washington in English spurs him on in the difficult and dangerous undertakings connected with the efforts of Venice to get free."

When Daniel began to appreciate his ability to determine to do and to persevere, his ambition and hope brought to him larger views of life. He resolved to learn in other ways. He took up school books and mastered them thoroughly, and he became known as "a boy who works slowly, but what he does at all he does well." He soon found helpers among kind gentlemen and secured employment in a bookstall. The accounts of his persistence and his achievements are as thrilling and as fascinating as any finished romance. He managed to get a college education, recognized by Padua University; he studied law and was admitted to the bar when he was twenty-two years of age. The Austrian judges would not admit him to their courts, and it is said he visited his law-office regularly and daily for nearly two years before he had a paying client. But his strong will, shown in his perseverance in the presence of starvation, won the respect and love of the daughter of a wealthy patrician. They had been married but a short time when the Austrians confiscated the property of his father-in-law because of suspicions circulated concerning his secret connection with the "Americani." That patriotic secret society was called the "Carbonari" by the Austrians, and Manin became the leading spirit in the Venetian branch. His will seemed resistless. He refused the Presidency in 1832, when revolution shook the tyrannies of all Europe and Venice fell back under Austrian control. But in 1848 he was almost unanimously elected President of the "American Republic of Venice"; and in his second proclamation before the great siege began he issued a call for the election, using, as Consul-General Sparks records, the following language (as translated): "and until the election is held and the officers installed the following sections of the Constitution of the United States of America shall be the law of the City." He was determined to secure an "American republic" in Italy. He lived to see it in

Venice. Statues of Daniel Manin are seen now in all the great cities of Italy; and when the statue was dedicated at Venice and a city park square named after him, he was called the father of the new kingdom of Italy. General Garibaldi said that when Manin made a draft of the Constitution he proposed for United Italy, he quoted the American Declaration of Independence. The general also said that Manin insisted the Government of Italy should be like the American Republic, and that it was difficult to convince Manin that a king—so called—could be as limited as a President. Even Mazzini, the extremist, and both Cavour and Gavazzi finally came to accept Manin's demands for freedom and equality as they were set forth in the Constitution of the American Republic. Manin did not live to see the final union, nor to see his son a general in the Italian army, but his vigorous will gave a momentum to freedom in Italy which is still pressing the people on to his noblest ideals. "What man has done man can do," and what Manin did can be done again in other achievements.

The normal reader never was anxious that the North Pole should be located, and he does not care now whether it has been discovered. Mathematicians and geographers may find delight in the solution of some abstract problem, but the busy citizen who seizes his paper with haste to see if Peary has found the North Pole has no interest in the spot. He would not visit the place if some authority would give him a thousand acres or present him with a dozen ice-floes. What the reader desires is to learn how the will power in those discoverers worked out through hair-breadth escapes, long winters, and starvation's pangs. It is a great game, and the world is a grand stand. The man with the strongest will attracts the admiration of the world. All the world which loves a lover also admires a hero, and a hero is always a man of forceful will. When we read of Louis Joliet and James Marquette in their terrible experience tracing the Mississippi River—Indians as savage as wild beasts, marshes, lakes, forests, mountains, burdens, illness, wounds, exhaustion, seeming failures—all testify to their sublime strength of purpose. Peter Lemoyne, Jonathan Carver, Captain Lewis, Lieutenant Clark, Montgomery Pike, General Fremont, Elisha Kent Kane, Charles Francis Hall, David Livingstone, Captain Cook, Paul Du Chaillu, and Henry M. Stanley carved their names deep in walls of history when differing from other men only in the cultivation of a mighty will.

Mary Lyon, the heroine of Mount Holyoke, used to quote frequently the saying of Doctor Beecher that he once had "a machine admirably contrived, admirably adjusted, but it had one fault; *it wouldn't go!*" while Catherine Beecher would retort that Miss Lyon had "too much go for so small a machine." But what a monumental triumph was the dedication of the first building of Mount Holyoke College at South Hadley, Massachusetts. Mrs. Deacon Porter wrote to Henry Ward Beecher: "I wish you could have seen Miss Lyon's face as the procession moved up the street. It was indeed the face of an angel." From that immortal hour when that little woman, peeling potatoes as her brother's housekeeper at Buckland, Massachusetts, suddenly determined to start a movement for the higher education of young women, she had written, had traveled, had begged, had given all her inheritance, had visited colleges and schools, going incessantly, working, praying, appealing, until the material embodiment of her martyr sacrifices was opened to women. All women in all countries are greatly in her debt. Men feel grateful for what the higher education of women has done for men. One cannot now walk over the embowered campus of Mount Holyoke College without meditating on what a forceful will of a frail woman, set toward the beautiful and good, can do within the severest limitations. Vassar, Wellesley, Smith, Bryn Mawr, and the thirty-five other colleges for women in Western and Southern states are the children of Mount Holyoke. One lone woman, one single will, a large heart! God sees her and orders His forces to aid her!

Richard Arkwright, Stephenson, and Edison in the pursuit of an invention, with stern faces and clenched teeth, work far into the morning. John Wesley, Whitfield, and the list of religious reformers from St. Augustine to Dwight L. Moody have been men of dynamic confidence in the triumph of a great idea. Neal Dow, Elizabeth Fry, and their disciples, urging on the cause of temperance with that motive force which they discovered in themselves, aroused the people wherever they went to assistance or to opposition. Fulton said, "I will build a steamboat." Cyrus Field said, "I will lay a telegraph cable to Europe." Sir Christopher Wren, imitating the builders of St. Peter's,

said, "I will build the dome of St. Paul's Cathedral."
General Washington said, "I will venture all on final victory," and General Grant said, "I will fight it out on this
line." When Abraham Lincoln gave his eloquent tribute to
Henry Clay in 1852 he said, "Henry Clay's example
teaches us that one can scarcely be so poor but that, if he
will, he can acquire sufficient education to get through the
world respectably." To such men log cabins were univer-
sities. Daniel Webster decided, at the end of his day's work
plowing a stony field in the New Hampshire hills, that he
would be a statesman. Thomas H. Benton, when nearly all
men supposed the wilderness unconquerable, decided to
push the Republic west to the Rocky Mountains. Salmon
P. Chase, from the time he ran the ferryboat on the
Cuyahoga River, kept in his pocket-book a motto,
"Where there is a will there is a way." Charles Sumner had
a disagreeable habit of talking about himself and boasting
of his learning. He was frankly told one day by James T.
Fields that it was a "weakening trait." Mr. Sumner thanked
Mr. Fields and told him that he had determined "to dis-
continue such foolish talk." "He fought himself," wrote
Mr. Fields, "and he conquered." James G. Blaine, in college at Washington, Pennsylvania, saw a student who had
been too devoted to football weeping over his failure to
pass an examination. Warned by the failure of this student,
James told his mother that he would not play another
game of football while he was in college. He kept his res-
olution unbroken throughout the course. When James A.
Garfield was earning his tuition as a bell-ringer at Hiram

College he resolved that the first stroke of the bell should be exactly on the minute throughout the year. The president of the college stated that the people in the village set their clocks by that bell, and not once in the year was it one minute ahead or behind time. Grover Cleveland at eighteen was drifting about from one job to another, and men prophesied that he would be a disgrace to his "over-pious" father, who was a preacher. Mr. Cleveland said in a speech that, "like Martin Luther, I was stopped in my course by a stroke of lightning." It does not appear to what he referred, but it does appear that he decided firmly that he would choose some calling and stick to it. He decided upon the law, and was so fixed in his determination to know law that he stayed in his tutor's office three years after he had been admitted to the bar, and there continued persistently in his studies.

IV

In a small town in western Massachusetts, forty years ago, a young, pale youth was acting as cashier of the savings bank. He was dyspeptic, acutely nervous, and often ill-natured. One day several large factories closed their doors, and the corporations to whom the bank had loaned money gave notice of bankruptcy. The president of the bank was in Europe and the people did not know that the bank was a loser by the failure. The cashier was almost overcome by the sense of danger, for he could not meet a run on the bank with the funds he had on hand. He en-

tered the bank after a sleepless night, fearing that the people might in some way learn of the bank's responsibility.
He was sleepy, faint, discouraged. An old farmer came in
to get a small check cashed, and the glum cashier did not
answer the farmer's usual salutation. His face was cloudy,
his eyes bloodshot, and his whole manner irritating. He
counted out the money and threw it at the farmer. The
old man counted his money carefully and then called out
to the cashier: "What's the matter? Is your bank going to
fail?" When the farmer had left the bank the young cashier
could see that his manner was letting out that which he
wished to conceal. He then paced up and down the bank
and fought it all out with himself. He determined he
would be cheerful, brave, and strong. He forced himself to
smile, and soon was able to laugh at himself for present-
ing such a ridiculous appearance. He met the next customer with a hearty greeting of good cheer. All the
forenoon he grew stronger in his determination to let
nothing move him to gloom again. About noon the daily
Boston paper came and announced the possible failure of
that bank. Almost instantly the news flew about town,
and a wild mob assailed the bank, screaming for their
money. But the cheerful cashier met them with a smile
and made fun of their excitement. The eighteenth man
demanding his money was an old German, who, seeing
the cashier count out the money so coolly and cheerfully,
drew back his bank-book and said: "If you have the
money, we don't want it now! But we thought you didn't
have it!" That suggestion made the crowd laugh, and in

half an hour the crowd had left and those who had drawn their money in many cases asked the cashier to take it back. The cashier now is a most successful manufacturer and railroad director, stout-hearted and cheerful. He often refers to the fight he had that morning with his "insignificant, flabby little self."

To appreciate one's power at command is the first consideration. A man from Cooperstown, New York, visited St. Anthony Falls, Minnesota, in the early fifties of the last century and laughed loud and long at the ridiculous little mill which turned out a few bags of flour and sawed a few thousand feet of lumber. It was indeed ludicrous. He could think of no comparison except an elephant drawing a baby's tin toy. His laughter led to a heated discussion and investigation. An army officer at Fort Snelling, who was a civil engineer, was asked to make an estimate of the Mississippi River's horse-power at St. Anthony Falls. His report was beyond the civilian's belief. He said there was power enough to turn the wheels to grind out ten thousand barrels of flour a day and to cut logs into millions of square feet of board every hour. The estimate was below the facts, but was not accepted for ten years. Then was constructed the strong dam which built up the great city of Minneapolis and represents the finest and most vigorous civilization of our age. Nevertheless, there still runs to waste ten thousand horse-power. In the first paper-mill erected at South Hadley Falls, Massachusetts, the horse-power used was less than one hundred, yet an engineer employed by Mr. Chapin, of Springfield, to determine the possible power of the Connecticut River at that point reported it so great that unbelief in his figures postponed for a long time all the proposed enterprises. But one poor man, determined "to do something about it," promoted a system of canals which now so utilizes the water that a large city, manufacturing annually products worth many millions, draws from it comfort and riches. Massive as are the present works at Holyoke, regret is often expressed that so much of the water-power still goes over the mighty dam and ridicules the smallness of the faith of those who tried to harness it.

Such is the intellectual force in a young person's mind. It is reasonable to conclude that no mind ever did its very best, and that no will power was ever exerted continuously to its greatest capacity. But the first essential in the making of noble character is to gain a full appreciation of the latent or unused force which each individual possesses. When one without foolish egotism realizes how much can be done with his wasting energies, then he must carefully consider to what object he will turn his power. Great wills are often wasted on unworthy objects, and the strong current of the mind, which could be applied to the making of world-enriching machinery, is used to manufacture some unsalable toy. The mind is often compared to an electric dynamo. The figure is accurate. It is an automatic, self-charging battery which, when applied to a worthy occupation or to a high purpose, distributes happiness, progress, and intelligence to mankind, and as a natural consequence brings riches and honor to the industrious possessor.

Forty years ago there was on the lips of nearly every teacher and father a fascinating story of a Massachusetts boy whose history illustrates forcibly the "power to will" which is latent in us all. I need not state the details of the life, as it is only the illustration which we need here.

A young fellow sat on a barrel at the door of a country grocery-store in a small village not far from Boston. He was the son of an industrious mechanic who had opened a small shop for making and repairing farm utensils, such as rakes, hoes, and shovels. But the son, encouraged by an indulgent mother, would not work. He gave way to cards, drink, and bad company. He would not go to school, and was a continual source of alarm to his parents, and he became the talk of the neighbors. He either was ill with a cough or pretended to fear consumption; the doctor's advice to set him at work in the open air was not enforced by his anxious mother. He was a fair sample of the many thousand young men seen now about the country stores and taverns. He had, however, the unusual disadvantage of having his board and clothing furnished to him without earning them. If he exercised his will, it was to turn it against himself in a determined self-indulgence. I heard him once refer to those days and quote Virgil in saying that "the descent to Avernus is easy."

One evening with his hands in his pockets he strolled up to the store and post-office to meet some other young men for a game of checkers. Under the only street lamp near the store a patent-medicine peddler had opened one side of his covered wagon and was advertising his "universal cure." The boy—then about nineteen years old—listened listlessly to the songs and stories, but was not interested enough to learn what was offered for sale. The vender of medicines held up a chain composed of several seemingly solid rings which he skilfully took apart. He then offered a dollar to any one who would put the rings together as they were before. The puzzle caught the eye and interest of the careless boy; as the rings were passed from one to another they came to him. He looked them over and said, "I can't do it," and passed them on. The Yankee peddler yelled at the boy, "If you talk like that you will land in the poorhouse!" The young fellow was cut to the heart with the short rebuke. He was inclined to answer hotly, but lacked the courage. After the other boys had had their chance to see the rings, he asked to examine them again; but he still saw no way to cut or open the solid steel and contemptuously threw them at the peddler and shouted, "You're fooling; that can't be done!" The smiling vender rolled the rings into a chain in an instant and, throwing it to the boy, said, sarcastically: "Take it home to your mother; she can do it!" The young fellow, ashamed, angry, and crushed, caught the chain and crept out of the crowd and went home, entering his room by the back stairs. He hated the peddler with a murderous passion, but despised himself and must have wept great tears far into the night. The next morning he sat on the side of his bed, gazing at the chain, long after his father had gone to work. That was a terrible battle! All who succeed must fight that battle to victory at some time, or life is a failure. He who conquers himself can conquer other men. He who does not rule himself cannot control other people. For the first time that boy was conscious of his lack of WILL. He was painfully ashamed. He could not again meet the boys, or the one girl who was at the post-office, unless he solved that riddle. It was far worse to him than the riddles of the ancient oracles or the questions of Samson had been to the ancients. No victory so glorious to any man as that when he rises over his dead self and can shout with unwavering confidence, I WILL. That young man's battle was furious and a strain on body and soul; he kept saying over and over again, "I will solve that riddle." He was sorely tempted by hunger, as he would not stop to eat. He determined to win out alone, and did not ask aid even of his mother. That night the rings fell apart in his hands and rolled on the floor. He had won! Life has few joys like that hour of victory. The rings had little value as pieces of steel, but his triumph over self was worth millions to him, and worth a thousand millions to his country.

The next morning his parents were surprised to see him the first one at the breakfast-table. He told of his solution of the puzzle, and said to his astonished but delighted parents that he had loafed around long enough and that he had determined to take hold and do things. He asked for an especially hard place in the shop, and entered that week on a noble, triumphant career, having few equals save those of like experience. His health became robust, his work became profitable, new business ideas were developed, and in a few years he controlled the inside business and far distanced all outside competitors. He said to his wife, "I will have a million dollars, and every dollar shall be a clean and honest dollar." In those days a million looked like a mountain of gold. But he secured the million and steadily raised the pay of his workmen. He became the sheik of the town, the father and adviser of every local enterprise. He was sent to Congress by a nearly unanimous vote. For eleven years he was a safe counselor of the administration at Washington and was a close friend and trusted supporter of President Lincoln.

One day in 1864 the Federal armies had been defeated by the Confederate forces and gloom shadowed the faces of the people. President Lincoln had a sleepless night—it looked like defeat and disunion. The danger was greatly increased by the abandonment of the scheme to hold California to the Union by building a railroad through the mountainous wilderness of the Sierra Nevada and Rocky Mountains. The chief engineer who surveyed the route said that it could not be done because of the great cost. Three great financiers had been consulted and refused to undertake the hopeless task. The great Massachusetts Senator told Mr. Lincoln that there was just one man who could do that gigantic feat. The Senator said to Lincoln: "If that Congressman makes up his mind to do it, and it is left to him, he will do it. He is a careful man, but he has a will which seems to be irresistible." President Lincoln sent for the Congressman and said: "A railroad to California now will be more than an army, and it will be an army—in the saving of the Union. Will you build it?" The Congressman asked for three weeks to think. Before the end of that time he asked the Secretary of War to take his card to President Lincoln, then in Philadelphia; on the card was written, "I will." What a startlingly fascinating story from real life is the history of that mighty undertaking. Now, when the traveler passes the highest point on that transcontinental railroad, 8,550 feet above the sea at Sherman, Wyoming, and lifts his hat before the monument erected to the memory of that civil nobleman and hero, he is paying his respect to the self-giving heart and mighty brain of the boy who conquered *the three links*.

It may not be necessary to multiply illustrations of this vital question, but no one who lived in the journalistic circles of Washington subsequent to the Civil War can forget the power and fame of that feminine literary genius who, as the Washington correspondent of the *New York Independent*, wrote such brilliant letters. The fact that she bore the same name as the Congressman we have mentioned, though no relative of his, does not account for this reference to her. She was nearly thirty-three years old when a divorce and the breaking up of her home left her poor, ill, and under the cloud of undeserved disgrace. Her acquaintances predicted obscurity, daily toil with her hands, and a life of lonely sorrow. Poor victim of sad circumstances! She had but little education, and had been too full of cares to read the books of the day. Her start in the profession which she later so gracefully and forcibly adorned was the foremost topic in corners and cloakrooms at her largely attended literary receptions in Washington.

She had been told by those who loved her that a divorced woman would be shunned by all cultured women and be the butt of ridicule for fashionable men; and that as she must earn a living she should sew or embroider or act as a nurse. She certainly was too weak to wash clothes or care for a kitchen. But within her soul there was that yearning to do something worth while which seems given to almost every woman. Few women reach old age without feeling that somehow the great object of living has not been attained. The ambitions to which a man can give free wings, a woman must suppress or hide in deference to custom or competition. As yet she has seldom under our civilization seemed to do her best or accomplish the one great ideal of her heart and intellect. While she has the same God-given impulses, visions, and sense of power, she builds no cathedrals, spans no rivers, digs no mines, founds no nations, builds no steamships, and seldom appears in painting, sculpture, banking, or oratory. She is conscious of the native talent, sees the ideals, but must hide them until it is too late. But this woman from the interior of New York State was an exception; like Charlotte

Brontë, she said, "I will." Like the same great author, she had her rebuffs and returned manuscripts, and all the more since at that time women were unknown in the newspaper business. But her invariable answer to critics and discouraged friends was, "I will." When in 1883 she said, "I will," to the great editor who became her second husband, the President of the United States wrote a personal letter to say that, while he wished her joy, he could but admit that it would be a "distinct loss to humanity to have such a brilliant genius hidden by marriage."

In an automobile ride from Lake Champlain to New York I saw the city of Burlington, Vermont, with its university, where Barnes had said, "I will." At St. Johnsbury the whole city advertises Fairbanks, who said, "I will." At Brattleboro the hum of industry ever repeats the name of the boy Esty, who said, "I will"; at Holyoke, the powerful canals seem to reflect the faces of Chase and Whitney, who, when poor men, said, "I will." At Springfield the signs on the stores, banks, and factories suggest the young Chapin, who made the city prosperous with his "I will." At New Haven Whitney's determination stands out in great streets and university buildings.

Chicago, Denver, Los Angeles, New Orleans, Atlanta, Raleigh, Niagara, Pittsburgh and a hundred American cities like them are the outcome of ideas with wills behind them in the heads of common men. If every man had in the last generation done all that it was in his power to do, what sublime things would stand before us now in architecture, commerce, art, manufactures, education, and religion. The very glimpse of that vision bewilders the mind. But the many will not to do, while the few great benefactors of the race will to do. My young friend, be thou among those who will with noble motives to do.

AFFIRMATIONS
FOR
PROSPERITY

Florence Scovel Shinn

M an comes into the world financed by God, with all that he desires or requires already on his pathway.

This supply is released through faith and the *Spoken Word*.

"If thou canst believe, all things are possible."

For example: A woman came to me one day, to tell me of her experience in using an affirmation she had read in my book. *The Game of Life and How to Play It*.

She was without experience but desired a good position on the stage. She took the affirmation: "Infinite Spirit, open the way for my great abundance. I am an irresistible magnet for all that belongs to me by Divine Right."

She was given a very important part in a successful opera.

She said: "It was a miracle, due to that affirmation, which I repeated hundreds of times."

AFFIRMATIONS

I now draw from the abundance of the spheres my immediate and endless supply.

All channels are free!

All doors are open!

———

I now release the gold-mine within me. I am linked with an endless golden stream of prosperity which comes to me under grace in perfect ways.

———

Goodness and mercy shall follow me all the days of my life and I shall dwell in the house of abundance forever.

———

My God is a God of plenty and I now receive all that I desire or require, and more.

———

All that is mine by Divine Right is now released and reaches me in great avalanches of abundance, under grace in miraculous ways.

———

My supply is endless, inexhaustible and immediate and comes to me under grace in perfect ways.

————

All channels are free and all doors fly open for my immediate and endless, Divinely Designed supply.

————

My ships come in over a calm sea, under grace in perfect ways.

————

I give thanks that the millions which are mine by Divine Right, now pour in and pile up under grace in perfect ways.

————

Unexpected doors fly open, unexpected channels are free, and endless avalanches of abundance are poured out upon me, under grace in perfect ways.

————

I spend money under direct inspiration wisely and fearlessly, knowing my supply is endless and immediate.

————

I am fearless in letting money go out, knowing God is my immediate and endless supply.

ABOUT THE AUTHORS

Born in 1874 in Iowa, **Christian D. Larson** became a popular New Thought and inspirational writer and speaker, admired throughout the United States for his work *The Optimist Creed*, originally published in 1912 as *Promise Yourself*. In 1922, it was officially adopted as the creed of Optimist International and today is quoted around the world.

A native of Ireland, **Joseph Murphy** (1898–1981) was a widely read and admired New Thought minister and writer, best known for his self-help classic *The Power of Your Subconscious Mind*. Murphy wrote prolifically on the auto-suggestive and metaphysical faculties of the human mind. His pamphlet *How to Attract Money* first appeared in 1955 and entered many editions.

ABOUT THE AUTHORS

Napoleon Hill was born in 1883 in Virginia, and died in 1970 after a long and successful career as a consultant to business leaders, and as a lecturer and an author. His classic *Think and Grow Rich* is the all-time bestseller in its field, having sold tens of million of copies worldwide, and setting the standard for today's motivational thinking. His piece "How Success Grows from Failure" first appeared in April 1921 in *Napoleon Hill's Magazine*.

Born in Missouri, **George S. Clason** (1874–1957) served in the U.S. Army during the Spanish-American War and went on to found the company that produced the first ever United States road atlas. He began publishing a series of pamphlets on success and prosperity in 1926, which were later collected and published as his millions-selling book *The Richest Man in Babylon*. His *Seven Remedies for a Lean Purse* originally appeared in his 1937 book, *Gold Ahead*.

Born in New Hampshire, **Orison Swett Marden** (1850–1924) was orphaned at age seven, and worked throughout his childhood as a "hired boy," going on to graduate from Boston University and Harvard. Marden published his first book, *Pushing to the Front*, in 1894, to great sales and acclaim. He went on to found *Success Magazine* in 1897, which had a circulation of a half-million readers. His *After Failure, What?* first appeared in his 1913 book, *Training for Efficiency*.

James Allen was born in England in 1864. He took his first job at age fifteen to support his family, after his father was murdered while looking for work in America. Allen worked as a private secretary with various manufacturing companies until 1902, when he left to devote himself fully to writing. He is widely known for his classic *As a Man Thinketh,* though he wrote many other well-received books before his death in 1912, the year *Light on Life's Difficulties* was published.

Born in 1843 in Massachusetts, **Russell H. Conwell** was trained as a lawyer, served as a Union soldier, and worked as an international journalist. He was ordained and worked as a Baptist minister before founding Temple University in Philadelphia in 1884. He is widely known for his inspirational lecture and book *Acres of Diamonds*, which he delivered before audiences more than 6,000 times before his death in 1925. *What You Can Do with Your Will Power,* one of his most powerful works, appeared in 1917.

Florence Scovel Shinn (1871–1940) was born in New Jersey and spent many years working as an artist and illustrator of children's literature in New York City before publishing her New Thought classic *The Game of Life and How to Play It* in 1925. Her *Affirmations for Prosperity* appeared in her 1928 sequel, *Your Word Is Your Wand.*